After World War II, a massive research project was undertaken to get to the bottom of invisibility experiments that were conducted aboard the USS Eldridge in 1943. Colloquially known as the Montauk Project, this endeavor sought to study the human psychological factors involved with invisibility and displacement from the space-time continuum. The psychic abilities of various individuals were monitored until time itself could eventually be harnessed and manipulated. Bizarre experiments then took place at the Montauk Air Force Station at Montauk Point, New York and have been popularized in the first book of this series: "The Montauk Project: Experiments in Time" by Preston B. Nichols with Peter Moon.

In 1992, Peter Moon attempted to corroborate that such a strange project did indeed take place. Surprised beyond ordinary belief — he discovered powerful and irrefutable occult factors lurking behind the entire scenario at Montauk. These adventures were chronicled in "Montauk Revisited: Adventures in Synchronicity" by Preston B. Nichols and Peter Moon.

Pyramids of Montauk: Explorations in Consciousness summarizes the events of the first two books and then takes us on an even more spectacular journey. The discovery of pyramids leads to an even deeper investigation revealing Montauk's ancient connection to Egypt and its position as a gateway between dimensions. A new look at occultism and ancient history will cause even the strongest cynics to pause.

▲

*C*over art: *The Temple of Montu*

*The God Montu looks up as you penetrate his realm
and gaze upon the secrets of his inner sanctum
in ancient Thebes. His patron planet, Mars,
shines through the gateway and reflects
upon the geometrical processes
which represent the matrix
of our evolutionary
development.*

PYRAMIDS of MONTAUK

EXPLORATIONS IN CONSCIOUSNESS

PRESTON B. NICHOLS
& PETER MOON

ILLUSTRATED BY NINA HELMS

SkyBooks
NEW YORK

Pyramids of Montauk: Explorations in Consciousness
Copyright © 1995 by Preston B. Nichols and Peter Moon
First printing, January 1995
Second printing, September 1995

Cover art and illustrations by Nina Helms
Typography and book design by Creative Circle Inc.
Editorial Consultants: Margo Geiger & Althea Carlson
Published by: Sky Books
                Box 769, Westbury, New York 11590

Library of Congress Cataloging-in-Publication Data

Nichols, Preston B. / Moon, Peter
        Pyramids of Montauk: Explorations in Consciousness
by Preston B. Nichols and Peter Moon
        260 pages, illustrated
        ISBN 0-9631889-2-5
1. Occult 2. Time travel 3. Anomalies
Library of Congress Catalog Card Number 94-69941

CONTENTS

PRELUDE

The Montauk Project: Experiments in Time was released in June of 1992 and has created a stir of intrigue and queries for more information ever since. *Montauk Revisited: Adventures in Synchronicity* sought to answer many of those questions and ended up providing an even more elaborate scenario that left us on the threshold of the occult and its relationship with the major mystery schools of Earth. The third book in the Montauk series, *Pyramids of Montauk: Explorations in Consciousness* digs deeper into the psyche of the Montauk phenomena and gives startling insights into the construction and drama of the universe. This prelude is designed to familiarize the first time reader who is new to the subject and also to reorient those who have read the first two books.

The origin of the Montauk Project dates back to 1943 when radar invisibility was being researched aboard the *USS Eldridge. As the Eldridge* was stationed at the Philadelphia Navy Yard, the events concerning the ship have commonly been referred to as the "Philadelphia Experiment". The objective of this experiment was to make the ship undetectable to radar and while that was achieved, there was a totally unexpected and drastic side effect. The ship became invisible to the naked eye and was removed from time and space as we know it! Although this was a remarkable breakthrough in terms of technology, it was a catastrophe to the people involved. Sailors had been transported out of this dimension and returned in a state of complete mental disorientation and horror. Some were even planted into the bulkhead of the ship itself. Those who survived were discharged as "mentally unfit" or otherwise discredited and the entire affair was covered up.

After the war, research continued under the tutelage of Dr. John von Neumann who had directed the technical aspects of the Philadelphia Experiment. His new orders were to find out what made the mind of man tick and why people could not be subject to interdimensional phenomena without disaster. A massive human factor study was begun at Brookhaven National Laboratories on Long Island, New York. It was known as the Phoenix Project.

Von Neumann was not only the inventor of the modern computer and a mathematical genius in his own right; he was able to draw on the enormous resources of the military industrial complex which included the vast data base of Nazi psychological research that the Allies had acquired after World War II. It was against this background that von Neumann attempted to couple computer technology with sophisticated radio equipment in an attempt to link people's minds with machines. Over time, his efforts were quite successful. After years of empirical experimentation, human thoughts could eventually be received by esoteric crystal radio receivers and relayed into a computer which could store the thoughts in terms of information bits. This thought pattern could in turn be displayed on a computer screen and printed out on a piece of paper. These principles were developed and the techniques were enhanced until a virtual mind reading machine was constructed. At the same time, technology was developed so that a psychic could think a thought that could be transmitted out a computer and potentially affect the mind of another human being. Ultimately, the Phoenix Project obtained a superior understanding of how the mind functions and achieved the sinister potential for mind control. A full report was made to Congress who in turn ordered the project to be disbanded, at least in part for fear of having their own minds controlled.

Private concerns that helped to develop the project did not follow the dictate of Congress and sought out to seduce the military with the idea that this technology could be used in warfare to control enemy minds. A secret group with deep financial resources and some sort of military tie decided they would establish a new research facility at Camp Hero, a derelict Air Force Station at Montauk Point, New York. This locale was chosen because it housed a huge Sage radar antenna that emitted a frequency of approximately 400-425 Megahertz, coincidentally the same band used to enter the consciousness of the human mind. In the late '60s, the reactivation of Camp Hero began despite no funding from the military. By 1972, the Montauk Project was fully underway with massive mind control experimentation being undertaken upon humans, animals and other forms of consciousness that were deemed to exist.

Over the years, the Montauk researchers perfected their mind control techniques and continued to delve further into the far reaches of human potential. By developing the psychic abilities of different personnel, it eventually got to the point where a psychic's thoughts could be amplified with hardware and illusions could be manifested both subjectively and objectively. This included the virtual creation of matter. All of this was unparalleled in the history of what we call "ordinary human experience" but the people who ran the Montauk Project were not about to stop. They would reach even further into the realm of the extraordinary. Once it was discovered that a psychic could manifest matter, it was observed that it could appear at different times, depending on what the psychic was thinking. Thus, what would happen if a psychic thought of a book but thought of it appearing yesterday? It was this line of thinking and experimentation which led to the idea that one could bend time itself. After years of empirical research, time portals were opened with massive and outrageous experiments being conducted. The Montauk Project eventually came to a bizarre climax with a time vortex being opened back to 1943 and the original Philadelphia Experiment.

None of this information would have come to light except for Preston B. Nichols, an electronic genius who one day discovered that he was an unwitting victim of the experiments. Working for a Long Island defense contractor, Preston was researching telepathy in psychics and found that persistent radio waves were being transmitted which were blocking the people he was working with. As a radio and electronics expert, Preston traced the radio signals directly to the Montauk Air Force Station and began exhaustive research that lasted over a decade. He acquired much of the equipment that was used during the Montauk Project and discovered to his dismay that many people from Montauk remembered him working there. It came to a culmination point when his cousin's husband insisted that he had been at Montauk. The two men almost came to blows over Preston's contention that he had never been at Montauk. Shortly after this argument, Preston began to get glimmers of a life he'd not previously been aware of. After talking to many different scientists and engineers who had some sort of association with the Montauk Project, Preston was able to put together what had happened. Somehow, he had survived on two separate time lines. On one, he worked at Montauk; on the other, he worked at a different location.

Preston's discoveries were confirmed when a strange man by the name of Duncan Cameron appeared at his door in 1985. Duncan had an uncanny aptitude for psychic research and eventually claimed to have been trained in this field by the NSA (National Security Agency). Without mentioning his own ordeal with Montauk, Preston took Duncan out to Montauk and was surprised to discover that he knew the entire layout of the base and remembered working there. Duncan was considered to be the primary psychic used in the time travel experiments and also remembered having been aboard the *U.S.S. Eldridge* during the original Philadelphia Experiment with his brother Edward (now recognized as Al Bielek).

According to the accounts of both Preston and Duncan, the Montauk Project culminated on August 12, 1983. A full blown time portal was fully functioning, but things were out of control and Duncan called together a group of people and decided to crash the project. While sitting in the Montauk Chair (a device connected to esoteric radio receivers studded with crystals that sent thoughts out of a giant transmitter), Duncan unleashed a giant beast from his subconscious which literally destroyed the

12

project. The people who had been working on the base suddenly abandoned it. The air shafts and entrances to the major underground facility beneath the base were subsequently filled with cement. The full circumstances behind all of this remain a mystery to this day.

Although an unauthorized video had been widely distributed regarding this story and several lectures had been given on the Montauk Project, no book was forthcoming on the subject. Different writers had attempted to undertake the task but were either mentally incapable of dealing with the subject or were frightened off one way or the other. One science reporter for the *New York Times* started the project but backed off when he discovered to his own surprise that the Montauk Project was indeed quite real.

I came upon Preston while researching an elaborate sound system he had invented and soon found myself listening to a spectacular story that was at least better science fiction than I'd ever heard. After several months, I decided to undertake writing *The Montauk Project: Experiments in Time.* That book was written without consulting anyone other than Preston (who wanted to protect his sources). Rather than do a costly and time consuming investigation, my strategy was to get the information out as fast as possible and use the book to gather other clues that would corroborate or eventually prove the existence of this incredible story.

As *The Montauk Project* was published further research and events continued that would indeed establish that there was a real scenario behind the wild information Preston was talking about. These were chronicled in *Montauk Revisited,* but the most spectacular of all these corroborations was the discovery that the Montauk Project was inextricably linked to the most infamous occultist of all time: Aleister Crowley, often described as "the wickedest man in the world". According to reports, Crowley himself had used the practice of sexual magick in order to manipulate time itself, communicate with disembodied entities and to travel interdimensionally. It was even suggested that the interdimensional nature of the Philadelphia

Experiment could have been the outward expression of Crowley's magical operations.

The startling proof of Crowley's association developed over a long period of time, but the discovery began to take shape in my very first conversation with Preston when he seemed to blurt out of the blue that he was connected to the magician Aleister Crowley. In an earlier life, he believed that both himself and Duncan had been Preston and Marcus Wilson, respectively. These brothers were twins and had been the first manufacturers of scientific instruments in Great Britain. In addition to being friends of Aleister Crowley's family, they had also been involved in a joint business enterprise with them.

All of the above sounded like one more wild story, so I began to look for any references to the Wilsons in Aleister Crowley's various books. None turned up. To my surprise though, I discovered that not only had Crowley visited Montauk (in 1918) but he had mentioned a "Duncan Cameron" in his autobiography. Subsequent to this, numerous instances of synchronicity between the Cameron and Crowley families were discovered, (these are detailed in *Montauk Revisited*), but I still could not find any references to the Wilson brothers.

The meaning of these various synchronicities (between the Cameron name and Crowley) began to be explained when I found out about a woman who called herself "Cameron". She is perhaps most famous for having been married to Jack Parsons, the world's first solid fuel rocket scientist and a disciple of Crowley. Together, they had participated in an interdimensional activity known as the Babalon Working (a ceremonial act which included sex magick and has been hailed by some as the greatest magical act of the century).

Through a further series of incredible synchronicities, I would fly to Southern California on other business and meet one of Cameron's friends quite by "accident". Soon discovering that she lived in West Hollywood, I suddenly found myself telling her in person about the Philadelphia Experiment, the Montauk Project, and the Crowley/Cameron relationship. Much to my surprise, she informed me that her real name wasn't

Cameron at all. It was Wilson!

It now became obvious that Preston's story about being a Wilson could not be discounted nor could his general credibility be denied. Perhaps more importantly, it revealed that some very strange correspondences were at work that had to do with interdimensionality.

I would receive an astonishing letter several months later that would close the case as regards whether or not the Wilson brothers had existed. It was from a man named Amado Crowley who claimed to be an illegitimate son of Aleister Crowley. Not only did he remember his father talking about the Wilson brothers, but he also provided clues which revealed that the odds of his lying about his parentage were nil.

Amado not only verified the existence of the Wilson brothers, he gave a spectacular account of his father's whereabouts on August 12, 1943 (the day of the Philadelphia Experiment). Aleister had directed a magical ceremony at Men-an-Tol in Cornwall, England where a large donut style rock lays upright in the water. According to Amado, Aleister put him through the hole in the rock whereupon a line of rough water ran from the coast of England to Long Island, New York.

For the most part, this is where the book *Montauk Revisited* ends. Amazing discoveries were made which showed that Preston was not off his rocker and that his general line of reasoning was valid. That is what the book was meant to do. Additionally, it showed that the forces which manifested the Montauk Project were deeply entrenched in the occult.

While *Montauk Revisited* did reveal a fascinating web of intrigue that is unparalleled in certain respects, it did not deliver many final conclusions. But even though we were left hanging at the edge of our seats with many unanswered questions, the book did accomplish something very important. It ushered us to the very threshold of the mystery schools, those secret organizations which have existed since time immemorial and have sought to regulate our consciousness and personal freedom. It is at this point that we open the door to our current book: *The Pyramids of Montauk: Explorations in Consciousness.*

DEDICATION

On October 20, 1993 Virginia "Ginny" Nichols, passed away at the age of seventy-seven.

The mother of Preston Nichols, Ginny worked as a grammar school teacher and was also a talented artist and musician. She also had a tendency to touch the hearts of those who knew her. One of those persons was myself.

Diagnosed with breast cancer almost ten years before her death, she was given six months to live by the medical profession, but she surprised everyone by hanging on. Her will to live was strong and despite repeated surgeries, she survived. This astounded her doctors and confounded everyone else.

I had met Ginny a few times and she was always very nice, but visitors were kept away for fear of possible infections to her. One day, she called me in to thank me for helping Preston with *The Montauk Project.* Although Ginny didn't necessarily believe all of Preston's story, she thought there was something to it. Preston told me the same day that he really wondered what was making her hang on. Based upon previous conversations with him, I speculated that she might have some information to release and that it might have to do with the Wilson brothers. Preston wasn't sure, but he did acknowledge that his mother remembered reading about the Wilson brothers when she attended college at Skidmore. As Ginny's illness prevented her from seeing visitors, the opportunity had never arisen to ask her about the Wilson brothers. Somewhat surprisingly, such an opportunity did come to pass a month or two before her death.

Preston and I had just completed an early morning radio

show from his house. Another show would be done later that morning and left us with a couple of hours to kill. Preston was tired and fell asleep while I finally got the chance to sit down and talk to Ginny. She was not in good shape but she was considerably cheerful. We had a long conversation and much of it centered around Montauk. I asked her about the Wilson brothers and she said that she most definitely remembered reading about them. She had been part of a parapsychology club at Skidmore and said there was a lot of information on them though she wasn't sure if it was in book form or not. The Wilson brothers, according to Ginny, had investigated their own past lives in order to find vortices with which to travel in time. In fact, one of their nieces was part of the group she studied with. There was absolutely no doubt in her mind that the Wilson brothers had been real people. It must have been very important for her to tell me this. It turned out to be the last lucid conversation she would ever have.

This book is dedicated to her memory and in the hope we may see her loving pattern in the future.

INTRODUCTION

Since *The Montauk Project* was released in 1992, many people have written to us about the strange mind control and time phenomena that they've encountered in their lives. There is definitely no shortage of these people. In times past, they would have been declared insane and forced to conceal their feelings and experiences. Today, these people are still very prone to being misunderstood and are often reluctant to talk. Most often, they want some type of help or validation of their experiences.

At the beginning, we attempted to answer every letter that came in, but we have long since given that up. Consequently, only the simple letters have a chance of getting a simple answer. But do rest assured that all letters actually received are read.

As a general rule, if you think you have been involved in a space-time project, you probably have. After all, the entire universe is really a space-time project in itself. The only thing that Preston Nichols or myself can do is continue to investigate and report on the phenomena of Montauk and hope that a shift in consciousness can occur.

At this particular juncture, the general public who have read about the Montauk Project are very supportive of our efforts. Unfortunately, the mass media has selected us as a target to ignore. This is their best defense. To decry us on television would only create controversy and get more people interested.

In the Fall of '92 and the Summer of '93, Preston and I

did a rather extensive radio blitz of stations all across America. Our availability for interviews was made known on the same channels that any top public relations professional would use. In fact, a full page ad announcing the 50th anniversary of the Philadelphia Experiment was taken out in one media publication. We learned that radio is still a free forum for the most part with various radio interviewers across America welcoming us in the spirit of free speech. However, the major media centers like New York and Los Angeles blacked us out. The talk show television circuit wouldn't even consider the subject for a minute, with two exceptions. Both of those shows had to cancel once their higher ups got wind of the show.

As it is written, *The Montauk Project* is not necessarily one hundred percent true. Some of it is based upon intuition and psychic readings, but its general premise is obviously much too close for comfort when it comes to the people who control the media.

When *Montauk Revisited* was released, there was no accompanying media campaign. Talking about occultism on the radio is not an easy task because most of the listening audience is in the dark (no pun intended). Time travel is literally a much easier topic. Again, this entire subject delves into subjects which the status quo considers taboo or best kept quiet.

Pyramids of Montauk not only digs deeper into why these subjects are taboo, but finally gives us some answers about the circumstances of creation. The majority of people who read this book will be reading this information for the first time and will accordingly be astonished. This book is written for them and is only meant to serve as an introduction to the subject matter herein. Most practicing occultists will find the information somewhat familiar but with a twist the likes of which they haven't heard. Hopefully, it will surprise them. Finally, this book is not meant to be or represent an official doctrine of any sort. It is simply an account of research I have done and information I have encountered. I hope it will make you more aware about the circumstances of your own creation and give you some answers you did not previously have.

PART
I

BY PETER MOON

1

RETURN TO MONTAUK

In the summer of 1993, musician Denney Colt was visiting Montauk after a year long gig in Spain. Having been out of the country and away from her home on Long Island, she had not heard a word about *The Montauk Project: Experiments in Time.* As she made her way to the top of the Montauk Lighthouse while sight-seeing, she couldn't help but notice a very odd structure on the bluffs of the state park. This was a large radar dish that was very conspicuous. Her intuition told her there was something funny about it and she expressed that she wanted to find out what it was all about. Two other women overheard her and said they had just been out there. Having been warned off by nasty officials, they were told that it was top secret and to stay away from the area. Denney became suspicious and determined to find out what this was really all about. She took a picture of the radar and headed back.

The very same evening, Denney made her way to the home of Lorry Salluzzi who happens to be a good friend of mine. No sooner had Denney arrived than she was handed a flyer that read "Montauk and Synchronicity" which gave information on a lecture I would be giving. Denney has had several synchronous experiences in her life and receiving this flyer on her return from Montauk was just one more. Consequently, she learned about the Montauk book and showed up at the lecture. Upon meeting her, Denney immediately told me about the radar and would soon show me a picture of the installation. This called for a trip to Montauk.

Preston, Denney and I headed out to the lighthouse in order to investigate what was going on. By early afternoon, we arrived at the radar installation. It was due west of the lighthouse and less than a mile away. There was a large trailer and generator next to a radar dish that was spinning. It was all positioned next to a large underground bunker which has since been sealed up. No one was at the facility when we arrived but there was a very lame sign which said not to go past a certain point. We didn't violate the sign but proceeded to circle around the entire bunker so that we could go approach the area from another vantage point.

Walking along the road, we were surprised to see a large flock of birds sitting on a telephone line leading to the base. Oddly, over ninety percent of the birds were headed in the same direction. They were almost frozen. We yelled and threw rocks to see if we could shake them up but only a few moved. The birds continued to sit there and didn't move during our vigil. Later in the day, Preston would video tape them flying in a frenetic pattern. They were flying in a circular pattern as if following a vortex or the like. It was incredibly strange behavior.

The road we followed led around to the other side of the radar. There was no sign from this angle and we could approach it directly. Once we got to within a hundred yards, two cars drove up to the installation. Six or seven people got out and some of them obviously worked at the facility. They were nicely dressed and appeared to be engineer types. An oriental photographer also accompanied them. As two of the men got out of the car, they hurried immediately to the radar. One of them made overly zealous gestures with his arms and seemed to be explaining the radar to the other one. It all seemed rather corny, and we had to wonder if the man was trying to convince us of something.

Preston approached the site and spoke to one of the men. He admitted working for the Cardion radar company in the function of Public Relations. Cardion manufactures radar systems and is located in the Long Island town of Syosset. The PR man said the radar was being tested and showcased for a foreign country that was interested in preventing small drug boats from coming ashore. He pointed to the ocean and said there was a small boat out there that they were testing. I couldn't see it. Even if I did see a boat, the area was ripe for fishing and it could have been a sportsman.

The PR man's story was ludicrous. Preston observed that this was a sophisticated piece of radar and certainly not one that needed to be tested for seeking out small boats. That type of radar had been on the market for years.

Upon returning home, I called up one of my friends and was telling him about the radar at Montauk. Ironically, he informed me that Cardion is one of his clients. He said he would ask around and find out what he could. A few days later, he told me that we had indeed been fed a PR line. The story relayed to him was that the military was trying to find a way of detecting militant Arabs in the Middle East. Low levels of radio active fiber were being introduced into the diet of certain Arab countries so that potential terrorists or soldiers could be picked up on radar screens. This principle is sometimes referred to as "barium screening". In medicine, one coats the inside of the intestinal tract with barium and it shows up on an x-ray. This was supposed to be a new kind of advanced radar that would pick up the barium.

I relayed my friend's story to Preston, and he was amazed. He said that the story doesn't hold water because even certain types of backpack radar will pick up people walking and distinguish them from animals. No such new or sophisticated radar was even necessary. It was obvious that we were being fed two stories from Cardion that were smokescreens for a secret agenda.

There were other oddities noticed about the radar. The PR man had told us that it was 3 gigahertz, but we would eventually find out that it was 6 gigahertz. An additional oddity was that the radar was pointed at the ground for some reason.

The radar also interfered with the viewfinder of Preston's video camera by interrupting the picture. Usually, this would also create an effect on the camera chips inside, but this was not the case in this instance. According to Preston, this indicated that it was not normal electromagnetic radar but something else. He didn't know what at this point.

After we returned home from our trip to Montauk, there was a lot of pondering over the radar installation at the Montauk base. It didn't make sense. Most obvious was that Cardion could have chosen a testing sight that was only twenty minutes away from their facility in Syosset. Instead, they chose Montauk, a location which was about two and one half hours away. Preston decided to consult his friend Klark, a man who has many family connections in the defense industry. Klark said he knew someone who was being assigned to Montauk from the Siemens corporation of New Jersey. His assignment included setting up a new radar installation on the inner base itself. Although this system could have been complementary to or an extension of the radar installation on the bluffs, it was in a different physical locale.

Those who are World War II history buffs will recognize Siemens as the same company that did all the electronic work for the Third Reich. This is just one more revelation in what is a continuing pattern of Nazi connections to Montauk. A quick trip to the public library would also inform me that Siemens acquired the Cardion corporation in the early 1990s. Everything now made a little more sense. I recalled the story of Norman Scott, an influential lobbyist on Capitol Hill who had almost completed a documentary about Montauk. His research led him to Siemens in Germany at which point he ended up with a mysterious heart ailment. After recovering, he begged off the Montauk investigation. There were still many unanswered questions but it was rather obvious that the historical German connections to Montauk were very much alive.

Preston then decided he could obtain more information about the radar by flying over Camp Hero and videotaping the entire area. He soon discovered it was difficult to find a pilot who would fly over the base. Finally, he secured a charter from the East Hampton airport. The pilot was anxious about going over the base and tried to end the trip after one pass over but Preston insisted he go back. They circled over the base a few more times and some footage was obtained that would prove to be quite interesting.

Upon Preston's return, he sat down and reviewed the entire tape with his friend Danny, a nuclear physicist. Danny soon had Preston stop the video tape. He was struck by the fact that there was a huge circle south of the inner Montauk base. According to Danny, this circular structure looked exactly like a particle accelerator.* None of this was taken lightly as Danny is one of only a small number of people in America who really understand the nuts and bolts of particle acceleration (he could actually build one). Without seeing further footage, Danny predicted what else would be seen at the sight. With one minor exception, he was exactly correct. We were being told that there was a real particle accelerator on the grounds of the Montauk State Park!

When you consider the idea that barium might reflect particle beam radar, the picture begins to clarify. Earlier, we had been told by my friend (who had connections at Cardion) that barium was being fed into people so that they could be viewed on a radar screen. This story didn't make any sense as people can be viewed on ordinary radar devices. But, what if "particle beam radar" had been developed? This would explain why they were trying out a new radar system at Montauk. Aside from any vortex monitoring or other possible esoteric activities they had going, they at least needed the hook up to the particle accelerator at Montauk. If it was ordinary radar testing, it could have been done locally near Syosset.

The Cardion radar was obviously not what they said it was. At least two lines of disinformation had been set up. One

---

* In simple terms, a particle accelerator is a device which creates energy by increasing the speed of nuclear particles towards the speed of light. A technical description of Montauk's particle accelerator is given by Preston Nichols in Chapter 35.

was to tell the general public that it was for hunting down drug boats. The second story was more technical but still flawed. They claimed to be using barium to detect people. If any part of that disinformation line was true (disinformation is loaded with truth if it is done properly), it was probably the statement that the radar would detect the barium. This indeed backs up Danny's contention that the circle at Montauk is a particle beam accelerator. We didn't have to convince him as he was sure of it. The fact that he is one of only a small number of people who have a mastery of particle beam physics made us pretty convinced, too.

We still don't know exactly what the barium is for. It is not to track military intruders, but it could possibly be used to track people and more speculatively, to lock into their psychic signatures.

Our investigation continued and we went out to Montauk once again and explored the circle in person. This time we were accompanied by Mike Nichols and Denney Colt. The circle was paved and it looked like it had been kept up. The bushes were trimmed to some degree but not too much. We found a patch of pavement that was much newer than the rest. This was exactly like Danny described. He said that there would be a paved area that would periodically be lifted up with a crane for maintenance purposes. Afterwards it would be re-paved. All of us who made the visit to the circle had reactions afterwards. Mike got very tired and disoriented. Denney was tired but also developed a red triangular blotch on her neck. I became extremely ill with a headache the likes of which I have never had. Preston was perhaps the most affected. He had radiation burns on his legs and chest. A doctor verified they were radiation burns but didn't want to go on the record for his own personal reasons. I personally saw a Geiger counter react when it was placed next to the burned areas on Preston's body.

The trip to investigate the circle not only substantiated Danny's contention that it was a particle accelerator, it provided some other interesting information as well.

Before we set out to the circle, Preston had set up various

radio receivers in an attempt to pick up any transmissions emanating from the base. He was able to monitor different transmissions, but as soon as he was fully set up, they would cease. As soon as he'd take down the equipment, they would start back up again. This went on a few times and was readily observable but was irritating. Preston figured the Montauk crew was toying with him and ceased the operation.

As we sat in the lighthouse parking lot, a local media person approached us. He took one look at the antenna on Preston's van and wanted to know if we were looking for aliens. He started giggling and thereafter I have referred to him as Giggles.

Giggles is a surfer and was getting ready to go down to the beach. He said he had lived in the area his entire life and that Montauk is indeed a very strange place. He said it all has to do with electromagnetic phenomena. Those were his words, not ours. Giggles acknowledged that the people in the town don't understand the phenomena and can be quite peculiar at times. He understands it and just goes about his own business without making waves. According to him, the best way to approach the Montauk locals is to go get a surfboard and hang out. If they think you are a local they might talk candidly about certain phenomena. Giggles said that surfing off Montauk Point had a very special energy quality. He compared it to Hawaii. I do believe that Giggles knew more than he was willing to talk about. He was certainly right about surfers being considered innocuous.

Earlier that morning, our friend Mike Nichols was surfing and noticed the Cardion radar. He saw some workers starting up the generator and asked what they were doing. One of the workers was friendly and said that it hadn't been functioning in the underground. They were trying to get it working. Mike was too stunned to ask any questions. He went home and phoned us. Little did he know that we were headed out to Montauk that very same day. He phoned us just before we left and we were able to connect up with him.

After Giggles went down to the beach, another surfer

came up and noticed Preston monitoring different electronic equipment in his van. He identified himself as Ray and asked what we were doing. Preston said that he was trying to find out what was going on at the base. Ray said he wished that someone would find out what was happening because he lived near the base and was often woken in the middle of the night by helicopters. He said they had been letting off huge amounts of equipment and people. In fact, it irritated him so much that he went down to the base and complained. The officer in charge was very nasty and an argument ensued. Ray eventually called the police who told him there was nothing they could do. Disturbing the peace is apparently out of their jurisdiction, unless it is curiosity seekers "trespassing" on Camp Hero.

We were later told by a town official that the soldiers on the base would have been the National Guard on bivouac training exercises. As the base had been declared a toxic and hazardous area (according to George Larsen, State Park Supervisor and also backed up by a Federal contract bid), something doesn't make sense. If the base is contaminated, it would be idiotic to have troops camp out in the midst of this toxicity. It was also out of place for the military to be so nasty to a civilian if they were just doing routine exercises.

All the events in this chapter serve to show that the strange goings on at Montauk haven't gotten any less strange. We were right in our element: a novel radar installation on a state park, reports of irregular and unfriendly military activity and the police acting helpless (just like the 1950s movie *Invaders From Mars*). To top it off, someone even mentioned the underground! What would be next?

2

A QUESTION OF OWNERSHIP

Neither Preston nor I were going to let the Montauk investigation slide after our recent discoveries. We soon returned to Montauk and followed the dirt road to the Cardion radar installation. Approaching from the west, we saw a man in a parked truck adjacent to the radar dish. Apparently serving as a guard of some sort, he saw us approaching and told us the area was off limits. He was not unfriendly. Preston and I turned around and headed back. As we walked back to the car, I pointed to a dirt path that led to the top of the bunker near the radar and asked Preston if he would show me around. After proceeding up a hill and through some bushes, we were surprised to find ourselves just north of the radar and actually too close for comfort. The man was now out of his truck and approaching us. There was no intention to hassle him on our part, but he had already seen us and was angry. Preston was video recording the entire scene which obviously angered the man even more.

"I told you guys to get off the property," he said.

Preston continued to shoot him on video and the man told him to stop.

"It's public property," Preston said.

"I don't like being on video. Now get out of here or I'll call the police," the man said. His anger was increasing.

"Go ahead," said Preston. "We could use that to show

harassment."

"What do you mean harassment?" he said. The man seemed genuinely puzzled.

I then informed the man that this is state property.

"Not this part," he said. "It's private."

It sounded like a poor bluff to me, and I insisted that it was state property. Preston then asked him if he could demarcate exactly where the private property began and the state park land ended. This was the final straw. He turned around as if he was defeated and would resort to being a "tattle tale". In fact, it reminded me of someone running home to mama. This is all the more ironic if you consider that the man was big, muscular and wasn't about to be thrown about by anyone.

As we had no wish for a further confrontation, we immediately returned down the path from which we came. In less than a few minutes, we were at the bottom of the hill. Suddenly, a state park police car made its way toward the Cardion sight but didn't see us. As we returned to our car, I noticed a hidden meadow. Inaccessible by roads, it looked like a perfect place for occult gatherings so I wanted to check it out and see if there was any evidence of such. It was awkward to get to as there were plenty of brambles and bushes between the meadow and the main road. I made my way to the meadow but Preston didn't want to fight with the bushes and stayed behind.

While Preston waited, he was no more than fifty yards away from the Cardion radar. He couldn't see them, but he heard the guard screaming at the police and telling them to arrest us. The police first wanted to know if we had disturbed the radar or the installation in any way. When informed that we had not, the police declined to take any action against us as we had not done anything wrong according to the law. The argument continued but went nowhere. I returned from the meadow and we went back to the car without any hassle.

Upon our return, Preston showed the tape to his friend Danny. Surprisingly, Danny recognized the man who had been guarding the radar. His name was John Zacker, an employee of Brookhaven National Laboratory who was at one time the head microwave technician. He was subsequently promoted to security and that perhaps explains his presence at Montauk. Danny had also employed the man in his own business at one time. After this incident, Danny called John but didn't hear back for six months. Finally, John got hold of him and was surprised that Danny had seen him in a video out at Montauk. He had no recollection of being there! Danny also reported that someone else had seen John Zacker at a restaurant out at Montauk. In that particular instance, Zacker didn't recognize the man and was nasty. He was reportedly eager to see the tape but left town and as of this writing has not had the opportunity to see it. We have all wondered, where did he go?

After our initial encounter with John Zacker, Preston and I stopped by a real estate office to see Carol Brady. She was mentioned in *Montauk Revisited* as having been very friendly to both of us and had helped introduce us to some local people. She had seen a stealth hovering over the base once and said the radar was still active. She knew something was going on at the base. We went in the office and asked for her but were told she was on a leave of absence. The woman at the desk knew who we were although I didn't remember her at all.

After exchanging some small talk, we mentioned our encounter with John Zacker. The woman then said the Feds owned the property and that they hadn't officially turned it over to the state. We corrected the woman and she became argumentative on that point. This was surprising. I told her to look at the tax map. She had one in the real estate office and got it out. We looked it up on the map and sure enough, Camp Hero was listed as New York State property.

"That's what I said," she said angrily. "It's government property. New York State government property."

Her demeanor was so overbearing that I backed off. I did express my curiosity as to why there would be so much confusion over the property issue. She was obviously getting more irritated by our presence.

"Go ask George Larsen!" she said. "He'll tell you."

I then politely explained that we really couldn't trust him

to tell us the truth because he was the superintendent of the state park and was likely to be involved in any conspiracy. Besides, he had told us the base was being demolished and was off limits. A month later, Cardion was discovered putting a new gate on the base. How does a radar company become a demolition crew? By microwaving the buildings?

The woman said that if we didn't believe George Larsen, then we should go ask some other man. She mentioned a specific name but I don't remember what it was. I wondered aloud how I could be sure that man would tell us the truth. She then peaked her anger and said in a very huffy voice.

"Then go ask somebody else – they'll tell you the truth!"

We left quickly but were amazed at the lady's reaction. Obviously, we were a threat to her reality. But she seemed to know more than she was saying. This would not be the only time we would hear that the Federal Government owned the land at Camp Hero.

A few months later, we would discover a newspaper article that would indicate that Carol Brady's van had been torched outside of Gurney's Inn of Montauk. This occurred within one month of the release of *Montauk Revisited* wherein Carol Brady's name was mentioned. She subsequently went to work at another location. We don't know the full circumstances and have not sought her out for her own protection. We have heard other stories of cars being torched at Montauk to serve as a warning.

As Preston and I drove home, we discussed the strange encounter at the real estate office. Why was the lady so adamant that the Feds owned the property? And then, why did she change her tune and get so bent out of shape? The subject of who owned the land was obviously a hot topic. She probably knew a lot more than she told us and likely let something slip.

Preston said that this was not the first time he had been reminded that the Feds owned the property. He was talking about a court case that was held on June 16, 1993. To begin to understand the confusion of ownership concerning Montauk's Camp Hero, we will examine that court case.

3

THE MONTAUK TRIAL

In February of 1993, Preston and Duncan took a trip to Montauk. Preston had already completed the video taping of what is now known as "The Montauk Tour", the only available footage of the buildings that comprise the inner part of Camp Hero. On this particular outing, Preston parked his van in a large flat area that is just north of the main entrance to Camp Hero. To the immediate east of the flat area is the base housing. These are homes that formerly belonged to the military stationed at Camp Hero and are now owned by individuals. Preston, Duncan and a third person went to a bunker that is outside the inner fence. On their return, they were outside the fence and walking back to the car when they were confronted by two officers who were state park policemen.

The policemen ticketed Preston and his friends but only after consulting with a man who was dressed as a civilian. Preston explained that he wasn't on the base itself and that he wasn't doing anything illegal. One of the officers said something to the effect that they would harass anyone who came nearby. As the discussion ensued, Preston turned his video camera on and let it dangle from his neck. Plenty of audio was recorded that could possibly be used later in court to fight the tickets.

In most cases, it seems that people would pay the sum of fifty dollars and be done with these tickets. Preston, Duncan and their friend decided to fight them. It was a matter of principle, not time and money. Further, it might establish what the truth is behind the ownership of the Montauk base.

On May 19, 1993 there was a hearing in East Hampton Justice Court, Suffolk County. The docket numbers were 93-4-345, 93-4-346, and 93-4-347. The judge was Honorable James R. Ketcham, the prosecuting attorney was Michael Brown, Esq. (Assistant District Attorney) and the court reporter was Elena McClash.

During the hearing, Mr. Brown indicated that all three defendants were charged with the same crime (trespassing). He also let the judge know that the defendants would like a trial to sort the matter out. Preston explained that he had earlier gone into the inner portion of the base to take footage for his video tape. He also said that he had gotten two different statements from the State Park Commission about what area is closed. A state park police officer had told him to stay outside the fence that says that the area is closed. Another lady in the Hither Hills state park office said that as long as they stayed outside of the area that said no trespassing that would be fine. Both of these statements differed from the policeman who ticketed them.

Judge Ketcham said he wanted to clear the matter up because other cases might come up. He also said that he used to fish in the area but wasn't up to date on the latest circumstances. Preston wanted a clear definition of where you can go and where you can't go. In fact, he was very eager to have the State Park Commission draw up a map. The reason being that Preston had heard from a lawyer friend about a law in New York that requires state park land to be available to the public. If one third or more of the land is not available for public use then the facility loses all its state funding. Preston was anticipating that the State Park Commission might hang itself. He had also done his own estimates and figured that the restricted area is definitely more than one third of the entire park area. It looked like trouble.

The judge was primarily concerned that proper postings

be done so as to adequately tell people where not to go. It was apparently outside the bounds of the court to order the State to draw up demarcation lines. Judge Ketcham said he would have the District Attorney bring the state trooper who ticketed them to the court and a trial would be held to determine their innocence or guilt.

On June 16, 1993 a trial was held in East Hampton Justice Court. The docket numbers and officers of the court were the same as mentioned before. I could not attend the trial as a friend had set it up for me to attend a Moody Blues concert and give Justin Hayward a copy of the *Montauk Project* (I received word later that he enjoyed it and that the next album of the group would be called *Time Traveler*). Instead, I asked my friend Mike Nichols to attend on my behalf. He would be my eyes and ears.

The defendants showed up early in the day for their trial. Not surprisingly, all other matters before the court were tried first. This was an apparent attempt to isolate the case so that other people would not witness it. I say apparent attempt because everyone eventually left the court room except for Mike Nichols. He was going to stay and watch the trial. According to Mike, the prosecuting attorney approached him and asked him to leave. Mike told him that it was a public trial and he had every right to be there. He was not bothered after that.

For purposes of expediency, Preston represented the other defendants and did virtually all the talking.

In his opening statement, the Assistant District Attorney charged the defendants with violating section 375.1, subdivision H, of the Park and Recreation Law of New York State in that the individuals entered or remained upon a property called a structure during the period, seasonal or indefinite, wherein this property or structure was designated by a sign or an employee of the office. According to Mr. Brown, "These allegations occurred within the town of East Hampton, County of Suffolk, State of New York". It is very important to note here that as a legal precedent, the court acknowledged that the property in question comes under the Park and Recreation Law of

New York State. Whether New York State actually owned the property was certainly not being disputed by the court or the prosecution.

Preston's opening statement (also representing the other defendants) began with his encounter with the policeman and lady at Hither Hills State Park. These are the same ones mentioned earlier who said he should stay out of the fence that's inside. This fence has red and white signs posted on it indicating the park area is closed to the public. Based upon this information, he believed that if he was anywhere outside of the fence that he was within the rules. He stated that he was wandering around the fire department bunker (outside the fence) when he was noticed by people who claimed to be state workers on the inside. They asked Preston and his friends what they were doing and were told it was a video shoot. The workers didn't bother them. There was no mention that they should leave.

It was then established that the issue before the court was whether or not the defendants were inside the fence with the posted signs.

The prosecution then called Officer Roland Walker to the witness stand. He said that he was employed by the New York State Park Police and had been a policeman for nine years, seven of them at Montauk. Officer Walker also stated that he went through the New York State Park Police academy and had training in Hazmat, radar, EVOC and paperwork.[*]

Asked to describe the signs posted at the base, Officer Walker said, "They are about three feet by three feet and they say property of State of New York, closed to the public."

Officer Walker testified that on February 5, 1993 he had been called by Donald Balcuns in reference to intruders in the state park. He then went to the entrance of the park and waited for them to return to their car. The officer acknowledged that

---

[*] Preston Nichols says there is a discrepancy in the court transcripts. He remembers Officer Walker stating that he was trained in radar while serving in the U.S. Air Force. If this is true, it is very suspicious and a very convenient omission from the court records.

they were not inside the fence when he saw them. He also stated that he issued summonses to the defendants. This was based on a witness, Donald Balcuns, stating they were inside the area. Preston concluded his questioning of Officer Walker by asking if he saw any of the defendants within the fence. The answer was no.

Donald Balcuns was then called to the stand by the prosecution. He stated that he lives at Camp Hero, Montauk, New York (he lives in the housing tract just north of the base) and that he is employed by the State of New York at Camp Hero as a master equipment mechanic.

Balcuns testified that the base was a military installation (at one time) that was fenced on the outer boundaries. On the interior, at another time, the 773rd Radar Squad was commissioned there which had an interior fence. He clearly acknowledged that there are two fences on the grounds.

The prosecution asked Balcans what happened at February 5, 1993 at approximately 4:45 P.M. He stated that he had been radioed by another employee that "we had seen some subjects in Camp Hero". Balcans investigated and saw the three defendants. He then radioed the trooper.

As an aside, we are curious as to why the employee radioed Balcans first and not the trooper. Does he also double as a security officer? And why would state park workers even care if someone was outside the inner fence?

Balcans clearly testified that the defendants were outside of the 773rd Radar Squad fence but were inside the outer fence (which encloses the Camp Hero facility). He said that he told the defendants it was a restricted area. They told him they were outside the fence and he radioed the park police.

As the trial proceeded, there was much discussion about the inner and outer fences. No one disputed that the defendants were within the confines of the outer fence and outside the confines of the inner fence. Balcans did say that the area within the outer fence was restricted. The prosecution seemed to be pinning their hopes on that point alone. Preston asked Balcans if there were any signs posted on the outer fence. He answered that there are no new signs, just old signs from the military installation. The signs say "U.S. Governmental restricted area."

Preston believes that this is a major telltale. Balcans says the outer fence should not be penetrated, yet the only signs are old Fed signs. In Preston's opinion, this indicates that there is still a Federal presence on the base. He believes Balcans was giving a signal. None of this was addressed in court.

Judge Ketcham dismissed the case because there was not sufficient or reasonable notice that the defendants were not allowed to go where they were seen. He also commented that the military signs are not state park limitation signs. The judge also said that if you go into the interior you have to have permission or permits.

At the conclusion Preston asked for a court order for the State Park Commission to define exactly what area is closed officially. The judge said he couldn't give that kind of order. He even said that he wished he had the kind of power and authority to give that. Officer Walker said he would look into the matter.

After all this commotion, a few signs were posted at the end of Old Montauk Highway at the west access to Camp Hero. They were just "no parking" signs. To this day, I have not seen state park signs forbidding entry to the outer perimeter of the fence. Judging by the report that the prosecuting attorney asked my friend to leave the courtroom, this entire matter seems to be a very sensitive issue.

In any event, Preston and his friends had won the case. More significantly, the court recognized that Camp Hero was a New York State park facility. If this is so, why did the police seem helpless when the surfer we encountered had an unpleasant confrontation with military personnel who were disturbing the peace in the middle of the night? And why was the military man he encountered so unfriendly? And what in the world was a private corporation (Cardion) doing on state park land? John Zacker had said it was private property.

I decided to research the ownership of Camp Hero.

4

THE INVESTIGATION
IS UNDERWAY

I set out to find out what was at the bottom of the Montauk property enigma and sought out the index to the *New York Times*. Unfortunately, the local Long Island paper *Newsday* is not indexed and that makes research very difficult.

I soon discovered that on February 6, 1984, an ad appeared on page B4 of the *Times* concerning Camp Hero. It announced that on February 8, 1984 the General Services Administration, a federal agency, would sell at public auction a 278 acre property at Montauk Point. It said that the site was a former U.S. Air Force Station. The ad was put out by Judith Hope, the East Hampton Town Supervisor and warned that such a sale by the GSA was unlawful because it would violate the National Environmental Policy Act (U.S.C. 4321, et seq.), the Coastal Zone Management Act (16 U.S.C. 1451, et seq.) and other law as applicable to the conduct of federal agencies.

The ad further stated that "On January 6, 1984 the Town Board of the Town of East Hampton acted unanimously, and pursuant to the authority vested in it by the People and Legislature of the State of New York, designated the entire 278 acres which is the subject of the GSA sale for 'Parks and Conservation' use. This action was based on sound principles of natural resource preservation and community planning and was necessary in order to protect the public health, safety and welfare.

"According to the East Hampton Town Code (Section 153-17A), the only uses to which land so zoned may be put are: 1. Golf courses and tennis courts. 2. Hunting and nature preserves. 3. Parks. 4. Recreational and beach areas. 5. Buildings customarily related to the above such as club houses, administration and maintenance buildings.

"Counsel advises that no houses, hotels, motels, condominiums, cooperative apartments or other residential, commercial or industrial structures, uses or facilities of any kind may be lawfully constructed or maintained by any party on the subject premises for so long as said premises are so zoned."

The ad further stated it intended to block the sale of the Air Force Station property and to uphold the current zoning of the property. We have to wonder if someone changed the zoning so that a radar installation could be set up!

Also on February 6th, Lindsey Gruson writes a special to the *New York Times* entitled "Officials Try to Protect U.S. Tract at Montauk". He states that "the War Department built a military base (at Montauk) camouflaged as a scenic fishing village on this isolated and vulnerable beachhead. No enemy ever tried to come ashore". He obviously hadn't read the various accounts of Nazis coming ashore at Montauk. Nor did he consider that perhaps the biggest enemy of humanity was residing right then and there at the Montauk base. The article said that the radar installation was closed three years earlier and the land was declared surplus. "President Reagan, concerned by budget deficits, ordered the Government two years ago to sell surplus land to raise money to reduce the Federal debt. Previously, unneeded Federal land was given to the states for a nominal fee, provided that they used the acreage for parks or other public purposes."

Interestingly, there is again no mention of using the base for radar purposes. Town Supervisor, Tony Bullock was quoted as saying "The parks and conservation zoning is very restrictive. It allows trees and flowers and that's about it". Almost every official at every level of government fought the attempt by the GSA to sell the property.

On February 7th, the *New York Times* reports that Judge Leonard D. Wexler of Federal District Court temporarily blocked the Government from selling a 278 acre former Air Force station on Montauk Point. He issued a preliminary injunction allowing the Government to receive bids on the property at a public auction but ordered that no sale be made pending a court hearing.

The following day, the *Times* ran another article on the base. It said that a Manhattan lawyer by the name of Jack Weprin bid $1.9 million for the property on behalf of Joshua Sundance Inc. Weprin wouldn't reveal what he planned to do with the property. A spokesman for the GSA said that the twenty minute auction had attracted two active bidders.

On February 12th, Jane Perlez writes a special to the *New York Times* which has Interior Secretary William P. Clark entering the dispute. He sides with the Town of East Hampton and writes to the GSA favoring that the property be preserved by New York State. His plan would allow the tract of land (known as Camp Hero) to be added to the Montauk Point State Park in return for 125 acres of state property being given to the Fire Island National Seashore. This was to be a land swap. Interestingly, his letter arrived at the GSA the day before the auction. It seems officials from all quarters were making a desperate attempt to keep the property out of private hands. Senator Patrick Moynihan also entered the fold. He pointed out a law to the GSA that allows them to transfer without charge Federal property that is to be used as park land.

On May 1st, we are treated to an article, again by Ms. Perlez, which says that Senators Moynihan and Alfonse D'Amato introduced an amendment in the Senate that would result in the trade of the federally owned Montauk land for the 125 acres of land on the State's Fire Island property. William P. Clark, the Secretary of the Interior, wanted the land assigned to his department by the GSA so that he could turn it over to New York State. Judge Wexler prohibited such transfer until he could decide whether the federal agency (GSA) had acted illegally in trying to sell the land.

Laura Durkin of Newsday reports on July 4, 1984 that Congress passed a tax bill which also called for the land swap referred to above. GSA spokesman Paul Costello was quoted as saying the tax bill "had clearly stated that the highest and best use of the property was for parks and recreation purposes. So the entire 278 acres will go to the Department of Interior, and Interior will make the transfer to New York State". Everyone seems to be ecstatic as the precious environmental property will not go to opportunistic developers.

The *New York Times* reports in the same week that the land swap is taking place and that a ceremony would be held on the following Wednesday to officially mark the exchange. It would be held on the Montauk property.

In what is thus far the most surprising aspect of this investigation, there is no article that I could find in either the *New York Times* or *Newsday* that marks the Wednesday ceremony. Newspapers live for that kind of reporting and you would expect a big article. No such mention was made. Did the officials walk into a time warp? Was the transaction ever made? Notice that the legislation was carefully worded (according to the GSA spokesman) that the Department of the Interior would make the transfer to New York State. I didn't know exactly how the bill was worded but for all I knew from reading the paper, the property could still have been in the hands of the Department of the Interior. One has to wonder if the entire press coverage was a manipulation.

But, I would soon see that the property crisis reaches much deeper. There is yet another claimant to the land which housed the Montauk Air Force Station.

5

PYRAMIDS DISCOVERED

After Preston and Duncan were found innocent in the "Montauk Trial", I was just about to finish the manuscript for *Montauk Revisited*. Before I called the book complete, I wanted to go to the library and check the definition of the word "Montauk" one more time. I was hoping to dig very deeply into the meaning of the word and pull a rabbit out of a hat. My surprise and intrigue at what I found resulted in my staying in the library for the entire afternoon.

The most accepted definition for "Montauk" came from Dr. J.H. Trumbull, an eminent Algonquin (the Montauk Indians were considered Algonquin Indians) student who suggests the word is from "manatuck", a name frequently bestowed on high or hill land, denoting "a place for seeing (or to be seen) far off" or "a place of observation". Although this was the most accepted meaning for the word, no one was going to dispute that there was no absolute certainty about the word. From the perspective of the Montauk legend, "a place of observation" is most appropriate if you consider looking through windows of time. But, the real intrigue and surprise I referred to above is not so much the definition of Montauk but the information I discovered while doing the research.

Going to the reference section on "Long Island", I first noticed a thick book. The author's name was "Wilson". I immediately picked it up. Titled *Historic Long Island* by Rufus

Rockwell Wilson, the book had no index and the table of contents was not much help either. I did find a list of "Plates" though and therein was listed "The Pyramids — Montauk". I opened to page 317 and found a picture of a pyramid shaped mound that appeared to be about twenty feet from top to bottom. There is a man standing near the base. In the distance, if one looks closely on the original plate, one can see two other such mounds.* Oddly, I could find no other mention of the pyramids or Montauk in the entire book! The book was published in 1911 so we know the photograph was taken some time previously. I had never heard about these pyramids or mounds. I will later elaborate on them, but will first continue with the process of discovery as I researched in the library.

The next thing I found was that the dialect of the Montauk Indians was lost. One account said that George Pharoah was the last one to speak the dialect. He was the Sachem or Chief of the Montauks and spoke his native language to John Lion Gardiner in 1798. It was stated that the name Pharoah had a long and important place in Montauk history. The Pharoah family were related to Chief Wyandanch, known as the greatest of the chiefs, and their name appears in many land documents concerning property disputes. Montauk had been coveted by the white man since his arrival on Long Island.

There was also a very famous Pharoah from the Montauks and his name was Stephen "Talkhouse" Pharoah. He was descended from George Pharoah and spoke an ancient language in addition to English. P.T. Barnum even hired him for a time and billed Stephen as "King of the Montauks". Interestingly, during his childhood he was bound out as a farmhand to a Colonel William Parsons. Parsons was considered notorious by some and was accused of enslaving the Montauk Indians. Unfortunately, I have not been able to find out any further information about him.

---

*The photograph on the facing page is a reproduction of the photo from the book *Historic Long Island*. It is possible that the pyramids were originally larger than they appear. By the time they were photographed, dirt and sand could have created a build up to fill the large spaces between them.

THE PYRAMIDS—MONTAUK

Next, we have to consider a vital question: what does all of this mean?

Suddenly, the pyramids of Montauk pop up in my research. Next, it's Pharoahs. This connotes a logical association with Egypt. Stephen Pharoah and the Montauk Indians being "enslaved" to a man named Parsons is also highly ironic when one considers Jack Parsons and the stories relayed about him in *Montauk Revisited*. Obviously, there was more synchronicity related to Montauk than could be logically denied. At this point, I was just beginning to see the tip of the iceberg.

As I continued to study in the library, I next encountered Thomas Jefferson (the same one who served as President). He was at one time very interested in the native tongue of the Montauk Indians and wanted to preserve the dying language. In fact, the matter was so important to him that he traveled all the way to Long Island in hopes of retrieving it. Jefferson reported that there were only three old Indian women who could speak the language. He dutifully recorded the vocabulary, alphabet and even composed some sort of dictionary. It was not an exhaustive work but was said to be a rather complete job considering the entire situation.

I was intrigued as to why Jefferson would go to such outlandish bother to record the language. It occurred to me that he was a Freemason and there could have been some underlying motive that would not necessarily be spoken of. I then read that he claimed to have lost the bulk of the Montauk language in the Potomac! Only a small part was not ruined. If it was so important for him to travel all the way to Long Island in the first place, why didn't he make a return trip?

I soon took my questions to Kenn Arthur, my friend who seems to know far more than he should, especially about Montauk. He was mentioned in *Montauk Revisited* as being highly critical of Preston's stories but also telling me that the real story about Montauk is far more bizarre than Preston could ever imagine. First, I told him about the pyramids.

"You're finally getting close (to the truth about Montauk)," he said.

I then told him about Thomas Jefferson and his pursuit of the Montauks' language. He told me that the tongue the Montauks spoke was known as Vril, an ancient Atlantean tongue. Kenn said that it was a later version of an even more ancient tongue called Enochian, the language of the angels.*

"How do you know they spoke Vril?" I asked.

"I just know," he replied.

My next question was about the name Pharoah. Why did the Montauk Indians have chiefs named Pharoah and why was the name so prominent in their history?

Kenn told me that there have been only two civilizations in the history of planet Earth that used the name "Pharoah". Egypt, of course, was one. That came easy.

"What's the other?" I asked.

"You should know that," he answered.

"Atlantis?" I asked, knowing I'd hit the mark.

"You got it."

Now, it all began to make sense, and I stress the word "began". There is much more to this entire scenario. I asked him if he could tell me anything further about the pyramids. Kenn said that there was at one time a series of small pyramids out at Montauk. They were supposedly white and appeared to be made of brick like objects. He said they were covered up or perhaps even taken underground, but he was not sure if the pyramid mounds I had discovered in the book were the same ones.

In *Montauk Revisited*, I mentioned my friend John. His father was once in charge of the Montauk Lighthouse on behalf of the Coast Guard in the 1940s. I asked him if he had ever heard about the pyramids. He said that his teacher once took

---

* Vril is more commonly known as a form of psychic energy or force. According to Madame Blavatsky, the Atlanteans called it MASH-MAK. This is a rough phonetic approximation to the word "Montauk". The earliest reference to vril that I know of at this time is in Bulwer Lytton's *Coming Race* which was eventually used as Nazi propaganda. While Enochian is known to have its own grammar and syntax, it is a hidden language and you will likely have a hard time finding out anything about it. Vril is supposed to have derived from Enochian yet is even more obscure.

the class on a field trip in 1943 and showed them all a field where Indian mounds had once stood. As the photograph in this book was taken prior to 1911, it would seem that the pyramid mounds were razed sometime between the two dates. The military (probably around World War I) has already been fingered by some as the culprit, but we don't know. In fact, I have been completely unable to find anyone who even knows exactly where the pyramid mounds stood.

My next phone call was to Madame X. She is a lady referred to in *Montauk Revisited* who says that the mystery schools have been monitoring Montauk as a planetary energy point for some time. I told her about the pyramids and she said that she was not surprised. In fact, it made perfect sense.

"Why?" I asked.

"Don't you see?" she replied.

I wasn't sure what she was getting at and asked her to clarify.

"Where else do you know there are pyramids?" she asked me.

"Mars," I replied.

"Exactly."

I recalled a conversation with her six months earlier when she talked about the relationship between Mars and Montauk. She wouldn't elaborate on it too much at that time. I would have to discover it on my own.

Now, Madame X was telling me that Atlantis, Mars and Montauk were intimately related. She also threw Egypt into the alchemical soup she was trying to feed me. What she was basically saying was that all of these locations, including other sacred sites that house pyramids and other geometrical structures are part of a grid system. This idea is not new and I had already heard many versions but none I had encountered were easy to understand in terms of function. Consequently, I began to study this area from a functional point of view.

For those who are not already familiar with the idea of a grid, perhaps the easiest way to grasp this is through the mythological correspondence of Atlas the Greek Titan who supported the Earth on his shoulders. Atlas was the son of Uranus (god of space or the heavens) and was the brother of Chronos (god of time). It is more than ironic that a book of maps is referred to as an "Atlas". The stories of him actually carrying the Earth were a metaphor for the idea that our planet is supported in space and time by a series of grid lines. The grid is actually a network of three dimensional geometric shapes that act as a skeletal structure of the planet and could be viewed as the bones that prop up or hold up matter.

According to Greek mythology, Atlas was the father of the Pleiades also known as the Seven Sisters which figure in the creation legends of almost all primitive tribes. For example, many Native Americans believe that they descended from the Pleiades. All of this is important because it implies that Atlas was senior to the stars and the geometric grid system that supports the Earth would therefore extend out to the solar system, the galaxy and throughout all of space and time.

One can envision the grid as a pattern for creation that some stellar or divine influence used in order to create a planet or the like. Such a grand creation would have to be balanced off at certain points and would eventually become a very complex ecosystem even prior to biological life being added to the equation. It is called a morphogenetic grid because it is constantly rotating in different directions and ever changing. "Morph" means change and "genetic" refers to the fact that it generates our universe as we know it. To try and chart this enormous clockwork of existence is an extreme challenge. The Mayans were one of the most successful. Unfortunately, most of the work that is available on this subject is not terribly clear and leaves one clamoring for more meaning.

As the Earth rotates around the sun, the grid lines of the Earth move at a different rate but they are all ultimately tied to the same system. From a human standpoint we can attempt to understand the system by at least two methods. The first is through mathematics which would include a complete breakdown of the intricacies of the grid. That is beyond the scope of this present work. The second method would be through correspondence and sympathies which would clearly embrace synchronicity. This second method would also include simple mathematical correspondences but would not go so far as to try explain every last manifestation (which the first method would be obligated to do). We will examine this subject a bit deeper later on in this book.

The fact that pyramids once existed at Montauk demonstrates that the location was recognized as a key point on the grid. This in itself suggests a correspondence with the pyramids of Egypt and Mars. There are also legends of a pyramid underneath the Atlantic where the sunken continent now rests. The very name Atlantis is derived from "Atlas" presumably because the ancient Atlanteans used the energy grid of the Earth to power their various vehicles. The Edgar Cayce materials discuss this and also how the Altantean culture settled in Egypt. In essence, all that is Egypt is believed to have derived from Atlantis.

The legendary connection between Montauk and Atlantis can be observed in the geology of Eastern Long Island. Originally known as an island throughout most of its history, Montauk is only connected to Long Island by a slender sand bar that has been fortified in recent years. Traditionally, one was said to be "on Montauk" when one travelled there or "off Montauk" when one left. Additionally, the geology of Montauk is different from that of Long Island proper. It is very much like an extended mountain that reaches above the sea. Some say it is a remnant of ancient Atlantis that didn't sink and that the Montauk Indians derived from the ancient Atlanteans. The royal family name of Pharoah is very suggestive of this particular theory.

Long Island is believed by most geologists to have found its current place from ancient glaciers pushing down from the north pole. Whether or not Montauk was part of this movement is debatable. If so, its connection to the north region links it to the ancient Aryan myth of Hyperborea and its capital city of Thule. The Nazis were fascinated with Hyperborea and its relationship with Atlantis. As there has always been a strong

German connection to Montauk, this is just one more correspondence.

We have now established, at the very least, that the language and legends of the Earth betray a strong association between Egypt, Atlantis and Montauk. Our next point to consider is Mars. Obviously, pyramids exist there, but I was surprised when Madame X called one evening soon after our initial discussion about the Montauk pyramids. She told me that
after our talk she had picked up a book entitled *CAIRO Biography of a City,* by James Aldridge. Of more interest to her
was that one of the contributing authors was D.A. Cameron,
one of the most knowledgeable Egyptologists of his day (circa
1890s). This book explained (amongst many other things) that
Cairo, whose real name is Al-Kahira, means Mars. According
to one account, the City of Cairo was originally to be called
Mansurya. A large contingent of slaves surrounded the perimeter of what would become the city. They all stood by with
digging equipment waiting for a bell to ring which would signal the time to begin building. Astrologers stood by as they
had chosen the exact time to start the project. To everyone's
surprise, a raven (the symbol of occult knowledge in the Native American tradition) rang the bell. The astrologers felt great
fear and decided to name the city Al-Kahira after the planet
Mars which was ascending on the horizon at the time. They
had a great fear of Mars because according to legend, that was
the planet from which people came down and conquered their
land, setting up pyramids and the sphinx.

The name "Cairo" is only one clear connection between
Mars and Egypt.* Madame X told me that I could find numerous correspondences if I looked hard enough. Consequently, I
began a somewhat exhaustive study to find more correspon-

---

* Cairo, where the Great Pyramid rests, is 100° from Montauk. If you break
the Earth down into a dodecahedron (a polyhedron with twelve plane faces),
there is a direct correspondence here in terms of pure geometry. As a further
matter of interest, Montauk is on the same parallel as Olympus in Greece
and the mythological city of Troy in present day Turkey. Mythological Troy
is north of Cairo and was supposed to be in its glory at the time Atlantis
finished sinking.

dences between Egypt, Mars, Atlantis and Montauk. I searched through various books and soon came to the Temple of Montu in Egypt.

Montu, also known as Monthu-Re, was the God of War in Egypt and a temple was built for him in Karnak. The God of War is an exact correspondence with Mars, the Roman God of War. Montu also corresponds to Montauk as a phoneme. A further example of linguistic correspondence is noticed when we consider that Montu was known as Mentu or Menthu by the Romans. This relates phonetically with Men-an-Tol, the ancient circular stone in Cornwall that Amado Crowley remembers from a ceremony on August 12, 1943.

Later in this book, we will examine different aspects of the Earth grid and the various locales mentioned in this chapter. What is important to realize at this point is that my investigation of the word "Montauk" resulted in my stumbling into the crossroads of some very interesting connections. There was a much bigger picture at work than either Preston or myself had realized when *The Montauk Project* was written.

The descendants of the Pharoah family were obviously a major mystery and an important piece of the puzzle. I continued my search in the library, trying to find out how they acquired that particular name. I discovered that white settlers often gave natives glorious names like "king" in an attempt to placate them, but this was not what happened in the case of the Montauks. There was no record of the Sachem Wyandanch being crowned as a Pharoah from the settlers and he apparently didn't use the name himself. The name would later appear in deeds and its exact history (until further notice) is lost in antiquity.

What was clear in Montauk history was that there were several land disputes that concerned the Pharoah family. To my surprise, there was mention of the land that included what would eventually be known as Camp Hero. It turns out that the Montauk Air Force station was constructed on sacred Native American ground!

This put a whole new twist to the entire situation, but

there was only one problem. A New York State Supreme Court decision at the turn of the century had declared the Montauk Indians extinct. I would consequently look deeper into this case and discover a real live human drama that only deepens the mysteries of Montauk.

6

THE MONTAUK MISTRIAL

After learning about the Montauks losing the rights to their property, my next step was to go to the East Hampton Library and investigate the court case. I was escorted by a friend who is familiar with the library and took me to a special room. One does not check out the materials nor does one even retrieve the books or papers themselves. The reference desired is selected from the card catalog and the librarian gives you the book or papers.

I recognized the particular librarian's name who helped me. It was given to me a year earlier by Dick White, the President of the Montauk Historical Society. He told me that this particular librarian had been involved in archeological digs concerning the Montauks but that she was very close mouthed on the subject. I didn't tell her any of this, but I did show her the picture of the pyramids and asked if she'd ever heard of them. She just laughed and said they looked like sand dunes. She apparently had no relevant information to share, but there seemed to be a definite attitude on her part. I didn't press the point. I then told her I was interested in the Montauk Indian court case. The librarian quickly produced a very large volume of the entire trial. It was very old. She put it on the desk and told me I could read all about it. I perceived what I thought to be some subtle disgust in her voice. It was not directed at me but at the entire mess. I began to study the court case and learned a lot about the history of the Montauks.

On October 13th and 14th, 1909, a "Special Term of Supreme Court" was held in Suffolk County, New York. The plaintiffs were the Montauk Tribe of Indians as represented by their chief, Wyandank Pharoah (a descendant of the Chief Wyandanch referred to earlier). The defendants were as follows: Jan Ann Benson and Mary Benson as executrices of the last will and testament of Arthur W. Benson; John J. Pierpont and Henry R. Hoyt as executors and trustees of the last will and testament of Frank Sherman Benson; Mary Benson, the Montauk Company, Montauk Dock and Improvement Company, Alfred W. Hoyt, The Montauk Extension Railroad Company, and the Long Island Railroad Company.

No one seemed to dispute that on August 6, 1660, the Indians sold the Montauk land to the townspeople of East Hampton. The Indians received a counter-bond at that time to occupy said land. To avoid any confusion, on February 6, 1661, another deed was made expressly to secure the Indian's rights to occupy said land. Note that each date possessed three sixes.

It must be stated and emphasized that in all of the agreements with the Indians and the White People, there was a solemn agreement on the part of the White People to forever protect the right of the Indians to occupy the land as long as they wished. The reason for this is intensely spiritual as Native Americans do not view property ownership the way the white race does. To them, the land belongs to the Great Spirit or God and cannot be owned by any one man. One can only act as a custodian. This great divergence resulted in confusion and negative feelings when Lion Gardner acquired Montauk land from Chief Wyandanch. When Wyandanch wanted to reoccupy the land, it seems that Lion Gardner conveniently "forgot" the arrangement. The term "Indian giver" arose from this dispute and has permeated the culture ever since.

The lawyers for both sides were well aware of how the Montauks felt about the land. The principal points of the Indians were stated as follows: "That their rights of occupancy have never been extinguished and that the deeds to the Bensons under which the defendants claim, are invalid, (a) because they were obtained in violation of the laws of this state; (b) they were obtained by the false representations that their ancient rights in Montauk would forever be preserved intact notwithstanding the deeds."

Much of the actual dispute centered around what happened when the property was sold to Benson. Two centuries after the townspeople of East Hampton had acquired the Montauk land, their heirs liquidated and sold it to Benson. The Montauks rights to their land was specifically mentioned in the deed and they held regular meetings on the sacred ground in accordance with their ancient rights. In actual fact, many of the Montauks continued to live in what were known as the "Indian Fields". After he acquired the property, Benson systematically went around to the Montauks and enticed them off the land by giving them homes in East Hampton or elsewhere. He claimed that the rights of the Montauks to the land was only a temporary arrangement. It was only a matter of time before the Montauks were scattered. Only after this point did rumors begin to circulate about the Montauks being a disbanded tribe. It wasn't really true. And, in fact, no one ever contested the existence of the Montauk tribe prior to Benson's purchase. One can also see the potential for manipulation when you look at the different companies named as defendants.

After the initial court dates, no decision was rendered. A dispute arose between the Montauks and their own attorney. He was concerned about payment and abandoned the case. It is not hard to imagine that the lawyer was paid off by a vested interest but no mention of this is made. After all, this was an official record I was reading.

On November 1, 1910, the court reconvened. This time the Montauks were represented by a new lawyer. A decision was rendered against them. On December 9, 1910, the headlines of the *East Hampton Star* read "Montauk Tribe Legally Dead". Notice that they said "legally".

During the case, the defense had focused on what they called the "Negroid" appearance of some of the Montauks.

They did not address the deeds, documents and merits of the actual case. There was even a report that a missing packet of crucial information wasn't considered at all by the court. Somehow, the defense convinced the judge that the Montauks were extinct as a result of intermarriage with blacks. The judge's name was Abel Blackmar which is rather amusing if you consider the proposition that people dramatize their own names. In such an instance, he would dramatize being "able" to "mar" "blacks".

The case was a civil rights nightmare. The *East Hampton Star* article even stated the Indians had a valid constitutional point on their side, but the newspaper said appeal was doubtful because other cases had resulted in land going to the owners. In my opinion, this is an extremely apathetic response: "the 'owners' are the 'owners' and that's just the way it is".

Wanting to find out what had happened to the case, I contacted Olive Pharoah. She is the oldest of the Pharoah clan and lives on the east end of Long Island. A very nice woman, Olive was glad to hear I was interested in the case. She told me a story that the court claimed that the Montauks were declared extinct because no one showed up on their behalf. This was definitely not true. According to that particular account, the judge said something to the effect that "Well, there are no Montauk Indians here. The case is dismissed". There were plenty of Montauks present at the court, but they were just ignored. Olive further informed me that the case was never appealed due to lack of money.

I told Kenn Arthur what I'd found out about the Montauks. He told me that there had been a systematic attempt to "degrade" them and their heritage by "forcing" them to intermarry with blacks. This was done through economic deprivation and manipulation rather than by supervised intercourse. The design was for them to become "the lowest of the low". Given the racial attitude of the country at that time, it is not surprising that blacks were viewed that way. What is more surprising is that someone wanted the Montauks out of the way.

After learning much of this information, Preston and I

visited Joe Pitone. Joe was mentioned in *Montauk Revisited* as the owner of the E.T. Company and was thought by Preston and myself to be involved up to his eyebrows in the Montauk Project. We updated ourselves with Joe and told him how Montauk related to Aleister Crowley and Jack Parsons. He was very well aware of who they were and conceded that we were into some "heavy stuff" as he put it. At one point, Joe began to talk about his home in Sedona, Arizona. We weren't aware that he had a home there, but I chided him.

"You're not supposed to live in Sedona," I said. "It's sacred Indian ground and you're only allowed to visit." (For those of you are not familiar with the Native American traditions concerning Sedona, this is a true statement. I was primarily teasing Joe but getting a point across at the same time).

My curiosity was peaked. Joe is in his seventies and is definitely not a "New Ager" as are many of the people who have moved to Sedona. Why would a military contractor who seems to spend most of his time in New York have a home in Sedona?

We then told Joe about the court case and Montauk being on sacred Native American soil. Much to our surprise, he knew the Montauk Indian case backwards and forwards. His knowledge is very far reaching in general but this seemed to be too much of a coincidence to be taken lightly. He told us that the Montauk Indians were extinct and that they could never win a court case for that very reason: there weren't any left! At least the court wouldn't recognize them due to the "black blood" factor.

It then occurred to us that Joe might have some answers about who actually owned Camp Hero. He obviously wasn't gung-ho about conceding ownership to the Montauks. Joe said that Camp Hero is federal property. We mentioned that the tax map said it was New York State property. He told us that the state were only custodians and held it in "guardianship" for the Feds. This is not the first time we had heard that the Feds still owned Camp Hero. It is one more example of the confusion concerning the rightful ownership of the Montauk base.

Many months later, Preston would hear from a friend who knew a current female member of the Montauk tribe. This woman told a story of a systematic effort by industry to deny work to any descendants of the Montauks. There was nothing personal in the decision. The idea was simply to strangle them economically so as to force them to join the military. The strategy was to force the Montauks to fill out an application for the armed services. There, they would have to sign up as "blacks" as there was no administrative way to include them as Native Americans. This would document that the people were actually blacks and not Montauks at all. This is just one more story of an attempt to deny the Montauks their native heritage. It has obviously occurred throughout the history of the property dispute. That it would be occurring today should not be surprising.

There is also another point to consider. On April 7, 1918, the Montauks were "made white men" by court ruling. The Montauks have not only been declared nonexistent, but someone seems to find it necessary to drive home the point again and again. The only apparent reason for this type of behavior is that someone considers the Montauks to be a threat. Never before had I ever heard of a court or anyone else going to such official lengths to declare a tribe of native people extinct.

7

THE MONTAUK TRIBE

It is now appropriate in our investigation to ask the following question. Exactly who was this tribe that was declared extinct and what was their heritage?

According to a book by Verne Dyson titled *HEATHER FLOWER and other Indian Stories of Long Island*, the Indian population of Long Island was about five thousand when white settlers began arriving in the 1600s. Different sources indicate there were originally thirteen main tribes. Each group had its own sachem (chief) who presided at tribal meetings and served as judge and executive officer. It is an undisputed historical fact that the royal or ruling tribe were the Montauks. Some accounts even suggest that the domain of the Montauks even extended far beyond Long Island.

As the white man began to arrive, the sachem of the Montauks was Mongatchsee or Long Knife. He had four sons: Poggatacut, Wyandanch, Nowedeonah and Momowets. They ruled the Poggatacut Indians, the Montauks, the Shinnecocks and the Corchaugs respectively. These chiefs formed a powerful and famous organization known as "The Four Federated Brothers". They were the famous sons of a famous father. It can clearly be seen from this information that all of these tribes were indeed Montauk Indians. The courts have considered them all separately in what could be considered an apparent attempt to denigrate the good name of the Montauks.

Wyandanch inherited his father's role and became the most famous of all the Indians. He was known as "The Wise Speaker". According to Dyson, Wyandanch selected Montauk as his royal headquarters. He also stated that the word "Montauk" means fortified place. Dyson goes on to say that Wyandanch built a stockade capable of sheltering five hundred warriors. Although the Montauks were a peaceful tribe, the warriors were fierce and highly competent.

Perhaps the most well known incident in the history of the Montauks is the wedding of Wyandanch's daughter Heather Flower. Known for her exquisite beauty, she was to be married to a young chief of the Shinnecocks in the spring of 1653. A great ceremony was to be held with elaborate preparations being made for prolonged festivities. Lion Gardiner, Richard Smith and other prominent Englishmen were invited.

In the midst of the wedding, late at night, a fierce group of Narragansetts from Connecticut struck down the groom and the attending young men. Heather Flower was seized and taken prisoner. Wyandanch's heart was broken. The warring chief Ninigrate wanted a ransom. Finally, Lion Gardiner, a blood brother of Wyandanch, arranged for the return of Heather Flower. Afterwards, Wyandanch granted Gardiner a huge tract of land on the north shore of Long Island. Gardiner would soon sell it to Richard Smith and the area would eventually become Smithtown.

It must be pointed out that the above account is the version of the conquering race. I have heard from different Native Americans that Lion Gardiner manipulated the whole affair. After all, someone had to tip off Chief Ninigrate that the Montauks would be sitting ducks during the wedding festivities. Whichever account is correct, Lion Gardiner had great influence over the Indians and this legacy carried on to his descendants. The Montauks seemed to have eroded amongst "the warm friendship" of the politically influential Gardiners.

Later in the book, Dyson quotes a passage from *Chronicles of East Hampton* by David Gardiner which refers to the Montauk tribe as being "reduced to a beggarly number of some ten or fifteen drunken and degraded beings". This passage was written in the 1850s when the Montauk Indians started to be moved out by Benson. As the statement is also false, it casts further doubt on the Gardiners being friends of the Montauks at all.

There was obviously another side to recorded history, and it was with this in mind that I approached the recognized tribal leader of the Montauks, Robert Cooper, or "Bob" as he is generally known. A retired police detective, Bob Cooper has also been elected to the Town Council of East Hampton (Montauk is within the political confines of the Town of East Hampton). I made it very clear from the beginning that I would not be asking him to accept the Montauk story or to get involved in the investigation. My intention with him would simply be to learn more about the Montauk tribe and to help them find the means with which to restore the rights to their ancient heritage.

Bob had not heard of the Montauk books but thought the story was interesting. As a policeman, he used to chase kids out of the bunkers years earlier and said that the underground seemed to go on endlessly.

I was also struck by Bob Cooper's appearance. Although he is dark skinned, he does not look like what would be termed an African American. His features would coincide with an Atlantean (based upon the legends of some of the various races of Atlantis) or Polynesian appearance. Bob said that he is 98 percent Montauk Indian and that his genealogy can be proven. The Pharoahs are his ancestors and his great grandmother was the last queen of the Montauks. Her name was Edith Banks Cooper and he remembered her speaking of constant threats and demoralization concerning the Montauks and their land. It was her dream to be recognized as a native of America.

It is Bob's intention to get the Montauks legal recognition and to restore some of their most sacred ground. His friends and fellow Montauks sometimes question why he would take on such a seemingly impossible task. The truth is that he is inspired by his ancient ancestors and sometimes wakes up from his sleep with a mission. It is not an easy task.

What I found most impressive about Bob Cooper is that he does not want the land so that the Montauks can sell tobacco and have gambling casinos. His goal is to synchronize minds through an environmental consciousness and, by example, to teach all native peoples to live indigenously. This is what the Montauks would use the land for. He has obviously chosen a position of leadership that is worthy of his royal ancestry.

Bob said that the Montauks have been displaced from their own world and that according to tradition, they must return home before all of us can leave to the next world. This symbology is in direct alignment with what I have discovered researching the Montauk Project. The sacred grid point of Montauk must be taken out of the hands of secret forces and brought to the forefront of the consciousness of all mankind.

As for the court case, he said they were very interested in turning around the decision that declared the Montauks extinct. It requires a lawyer who understands Indian law and is not interested in the case for his own profit. At this point, such a lawyer has not been forthcoming. He also told us that a top Indian lawyer once said "The best case in the nation is that of the Montauks". Unfortunately, this lawyer has not been able to take the case on for personal reasons.

If anyone is interested in contributing to this cause, they can write to the Friends of the Pharoahs, care of Bob Cooper, PO Box 126, East Hampton, New York 11937-0126.

Perhaps the most intriguing thing I learned from talking to Bob Cooper is the Non-Intercourse Act of 1793. This legislation was passed early in American history and stated that any land that was owned by the Federal Government, upon being dispossessed, reverts back to the original owner(s). This makes the entire question of who owns Camp Hero much more complicated. If the Government were at any point to give up ownership of the land, it should revert to the Montauk Tribe. Unfortunately, the Montauks have been declared extinct by the New York State Supreme Court. If this case were ever overturned, the Montauks claim to their land would be very hard to dispute.

The next order of business was to search out the deed for Camp Hero and discover who actually owned the land.

BOTTOMLESS POND

Above is a triangular shaped pond
situated to the northeast and just on the other side of
Industrial Road from Fort Pond. At first glance it appears to be an
extension of that body of water, however several people
have reported that it is bottomless. No one disputes
that it is very deep. There is an ancient legend
that a member of the Montauk Nation whose reputation
was ruined and life forfeited by some act of crime,
fled to this location, placed his foot on a rock,
and sprang forward into a valley which opened to received him.
As the earth closed behind him, a spring gushed forth
which never ceased. A permanent footprint was
left on the rock which has since been removed from the area.
There were reportedly three such rocks at Montauk,
sometimes identified as the "Devil's Hoofprint".
It has been speculated that the "ceaseless spring"
became this bottomless pond.

8

THE DEED IS FOUND

If we review Chapter Four, it states that the Department of the Interior was to have received the Camp Hero grounds and then turn it over to the State of New York as park land. The reason for this would seem too obvious. If the Department of the Interior is in possession of the land, it still belongs to the United States Government. If it is officially turned over to the state, the land has become dispossessed and reverts back to the original owners, the Montauk tribe.

Of course, there is no question that Camp Hero is currently under supervision of the New York State Park Commission. However, if that were truly the case, there would be no secret projects going on and the entire area would not be so guarded.

Councilman Cooper told me that there should be a deed on file in the Office of the County Clerk in Riverhead, New York. I made the trip to Riverhead and parked in the county parking lot. Just in front of me and to the right was a car of identical make, color and year. A woman had just parked and was getting out. I noticed that her license plate included the numbers "666". I thought of asking her about her license number but decided against it. Eventually on returning to my own car, I noticed my own mileage counter said 066.6 exactly. I realized that I had travelled that exact amount of miles from my house. The numbers "666" appearing is very ironic when you consider that two deeds were signed for the property under consideration on August 6, 1660 and February 6, 1661.

I then went into the County Clerk's office, asked questions and proceeded to find the deed of ownership for the land known as Camp Hero. For those who are interested and want to look up the deed themselves, it can be found in Liber 9670 beginning on page 153 and ending on page 161 of the property records of Suffolk County, New York.

The deed is worded "Quitclaim Deed" and the document does not exactly show itself to be the transfer of property we were led to believe would happen from the newspaper accounts. In July, *Long Island Newsday* reported there would be a deed ceremony the following week. This particular deed was not even signed until September 10, 1984 by the U.S. Government's representative whose signature appears to be James W. Coleman Jr., Regional Director of the National Park Service, Mid-Atlantic Region, 143 Third Street, Philadelphia, Pennsylvania. The representative for New York State did not accept the transfer legally until October 16, 1984.

The deed specifically states that the United States of America grants the property "for public park or public recreation purposes in perpetuity by the People of the State of New York". But, it reserves the right to take back the property at a moment's notice with particular regard to the defense of the United States. It is specifically a "Quitclaim Deed" and not an actual transfer of property. The deed also stipulates that the United States shall reserve all mining rights to the property together with the right to access the land for such purpose. This gives them carte blanche to maintain a "legal" underground facility. Further, the deed states that amendments and stipulations can be added to by either party and with approval, the entire nature of the agreements in the deed are subject to change. And, if the State does not run the park in accordance with the wishes of the Federal Government, the United States can move in and take over.

Before publication, I showed this chapter to a real estate professional who didn't believe me. She said a quitclaim deed

SIGN AT CAMP HERO

The above sign says
"CAMP HERO SECTION OF MONTAUK POINT
STATE PARK. THIS LAND WAS DONATED
BY THE FEDERAL GOVERNMENT".
Webster's New World Dictionary defines donate as
"to give, especially to some philanthropic or
religious cause; contribute".

means the conveyor relinquishes all claim to the property and deeds it over absolutely and irrevocably. Something like mining rights could be an exception but not a change of agreements. I must add that I have not exaggerated one bit. Anyone is invited to check the deed out for themselves.

Obviously, this arrangement is very cozy for running a clandestine secret project. The entire affair was reported in the press as a transfer of property. New York State would give part of Fire Island for the Fire Island National Seashore. In return, the U.S. would give Camp Hero to New York State. If one reads all the news articles I have reported on, they reveal an ingenious manner with which to manipulate the public's opinion. Because the deed is technically a quitclaim, with reservations and stipulations, it does not give an absolute and irrevocable transfer of property to New York State. If it did, the property would technically belong to the Montauk tribe. It should be noted that although the Montauks were declared extinct by New York State, there is no such federal decision against them.

What I have said here is not a complete expert legal opinion but it gives the general merits of the situation. It is highly interesting that Joe Pitone was the only one who seemed to know the exact legal arrangement of Camp Hero. He had told us that the State of New York was acting as custodian for the Feds. Although he doesn't claim any involvement in Montauk, it is very odd that he would know the circumstances so well.

Of course, none of this information is a deterrent to the Montauks getting their sacred ground back. Technically, if the Montauks are recognized for what they truly are, the property should revert to them despite any of the information stipulated in the quitclaim deed.

It is imperative that the Montauks receive help in overturning their own case as it has been speculated that someone in the Government might try and instigate legislation that would block the retroactive aspect of the 1793 legislation requiring all property dispossessed by the Government to revert to the original owners.

9

THE MONTAUK SHAMAN

The deed for the Montauks' property is a very important issue and while not in any way trying to lessen that cause, the legacy of the Pharoah's and their ancestry forces us to look at even deeper implications.

As the recognized tribal leader of the Montauks, Bob Cooper had led me to the deed and the true history of his people. Next, he would do me an even greater service by arranging an introduction to Sharon Jackson, the Shaman of the Montauks who is a blood descendant of the Pharoahs and is also known as Queen of the Montauks.

In addition to the special legacy that has been handed down to her as Shaman, Sharon works as a minister and also runs an association to help children with AIDS. When we met, she told me that the Montauks had descended from the Leni Lenape of the Delaware Valley, a great confederation that included thirty-two subdivisions. According to tradition, the Leni Lenape "always were". The Montauks were one of three main divisions that inhabited what is now the New York metropolitan area. The Matinnecocks occupied western Long Island and parts of New Jersey and their totem animal was the turkey . The Unami lived in the areas of Brooklyn, Manhattan and along the Hudson River. Their totem was the wolf. The Montauks were the chief tribe and they filled up the rest of Long Island. The turtle was their sacred animal.

Sharon explained that the Montauks had been very careful to preserve their heritage all along. The action of the court was hurtful and negative but it by no means was a death blow. Hundreds of years ago, the Montauks split into two primary locales on Long Island. There was the Freetown branch in the Southampton area and also the Eastville branch who settled towards the middle of Long Island. The Freetown Montauks consisted of the Pharoah family proper. In other words, these people carried the Pharoah name. The Eastville Montauks were definitely related, but they were not recognized as Montauks because they didn't live near the area after having been systematically moved out. According to Sharon, the Eastville Montauks were more concerned with their spiritual heritage.

It is impressive to listen to the Shaman talk of the preservation instincts of her race. They have always been a quiet and unobtrusive people and have tended to intermarry within the tribe, primarily for sheer survival of their heritage. Extensive geneological records have been kept to back this up and these should prove binding in any future court cases.

Both Sharon Jackson and Robert Cooper told me that the entire history of the Montauks was being reconstructed and rewritten by Professor John Strong of Southampton College. His work is extensive and documented and I am told that he is supremely confident the Montauks will win their case. Of course, this doesn't guarantee anything. The data may back up the Montauks, but all of us must ensure that no shifty business occurs. Anything can and might be tried.

Since Preston and I met with Robert Cooper and befriended his cause, he has received scathing attacks in the local press that have erroneously called him a "Black Native American" and have otherwise sought to discredit him. After asking that accusations (from different sources) of police corruption be looked into, a local press article ran suggesting that he resign from the Town Council and give up his pension as a retired policeman. It was said his actions were irresponsible. Asking Bob about the matter, he said that he had made no accusations against anybody. He only asked that they be looked into. I relay all of this so you will know that there is opposition to the Montauks and their claim to their rightful heritage. Any of you in the reading audience who can help are encouraged to do so.

As I spoke to the Shaman, it was a relief for me to hear that the Montauks were enough together to put up a fight, but I was also eager to find out if Sharon had heard of the Montauk Pyramids. Bob Cooper had not. I showed Sharon a copy of the photograph and she gave a most interesting response. She said that native peoples seldom build a structure so that you will automatically know what it is. The mysteries will lie in a different place. She noticed that the pyramids are in a line and that is unusual for a native structure. Normally, mounds are in a circle or half moon formation. According to her, this symbolized progression and indicated they were not of the Earth.

I then told her the legend that the mounds covered small block pyramids that were made of some sort of white stone. She then wondered if they could have been constructed from parts of Council Rock. Not knowing what Council Rock was, I asked Sharon to explain it.

A large white rock with caramel streaks and underside, it appears to be made of milky quartz. Now situated in the midst of a cemetary near Montauk Manor, it served the Montauks as their major meeting place for centuries. Sharon told me that geologists have determined that the rock is not indigenous to the Montauk area but would likely come from Mexico. It is too large to have been put aboard an ancient ship and adds one more piece of mystery to the enigma that is Montauk.

While the puzzle of Council Rock remains unsolved at this writing, what the Montauk Shaman said about the mysteries lying in a different place than the pyramids is noteworthy. With the help of at least one brilliant scholar, we will now examine Montauk's Turtle Cove.

COUNCIL ROCK

Serving as a meeting place for the Montauk Nation
for many generations, Council Rock was moved from its original
location when the Fort Hill Cemetery was established.
How the rock was originally deposited at Montauk
remains a mystery to this day.

MONTAUK COMMUNITY CHURCH

Located on Montauk Highway, just east of the town,
the Montauk Community Church was built with stones taken from
the Montauks' sacred burial grounds.

10

TURTLE COVE

Located a few miles southeast of the transmitter building, Turtle Cove is just a short walk west of the Montauk lighthouse. Although many Native Americans are not aware of it, there is a tradition in their culture that the world originated from Turtle Cove. Whether the origin of Earth was at Montauk or not is quite debatable, but there were definitely some people who espoused this belief. If one looks deeper into the traditions of different Native American tribes, there is definitely a common belief that the turtle is at the source point of the universe.

The above idea is obviously a mythological account and usually not a very clear one in most of the renditions I have read. Many people have heard stories about the Earth being supported on the backs of a series of different turtles. At first glance, a turtle holding up the globe would seem totally absurd. If we dig deeper into the mythology, we learn that this particular myth is a metaphor for a principle that has a very deep meaning.

In order that you understand this metaphor, it is necessary that I introduce you to the MERU Foundation, a research group which has been recovering lost knowledge that was previously only for mystery school initiates. Some of the most spectacular work of the MERU Foundation is the decoding of the Hebrew alphabet. This began in 1968 when a man by the name of Stan Tenen just happened to be looking at the beginning of a Hebrew version of the Book of Genesis. As Stan didn't read Hebrew, the text made no sense to him. But, as he is very gifted in the area of pattern recognition, he noticed there was something peculiar about the sequence of the letters. There was some sort of symmetrical relationship, but he wasn't sure what it was. Consequently, a ten year quest began to find the answer.

Finally, after reading every book he could find and trying all sorts of sophisticated mathematical techniques, Stan finally resorted to doing the simplest thing he could. He took the first verse of Genesis and wrote each letter out, one each, on a bead chain and curled the bead chain around until the identical letter-beads lined up with each other. The result was a form that looked like a two dimensional pyramid (see Figure 1).

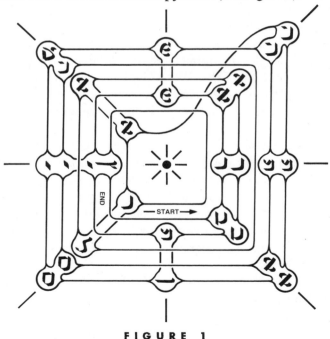

FIGURE 1

Bead-chain wrapping of letters in Genesis 1:1, showing form created by matching letters. Copyright © 1989 by Stan Tenen

80

All of this not only suggests the sacred geometrical nature of the pyramid, it reveals possible synchronicity between the Hebrew alphabet and sacred geometry. But, this was just the first step in Stan Tenen's brilliant discovery. Further work would show that the alphabet correlated with other geometrical shapes.

Perhaps the most remarkable discovery he made was that when he paired all the letters and then mathematically reduced that shape to the most compact and elegant form he could, he ended up with a very unusual form. It is best described as a special sort of three dimensional vortex. What was so astonishing about this endeavor was that if you looked at the vortex from twenty-seven different angles, you would see all twenty-seven letters of the Hebrew alphabet. Similarly if you were to hold a light behind a solid rendition of the vortex and move around it from twenty-seven different angles, you would see all the Hebrew letters in shadow form. (See Figure 4).

Stan arrived at this vortex shape by pairing the letters together but that is not the only way the shape could be arrived at. For this next step, we will consider a torus or doughnut. For those of you who remember reading Appendix F of *The Montauk Project*, the entire universe can be likened to the shape of a doughnut. This idea is commonly accepted in the world of physics and is not any great revelation in itself. Stan realized that you can create a torus by taking a flat piece of paper and rolling it into a tube, then connecting the two ends (actually, paper does not obligingly shrink and stretch to make a perfect doughnut but the idea will serve). The reason we use paper in this example is that we are going to insert the seven colors of the spectrum into our equation. Before we make the torus mentioned above, we are going to lay out seven colors on a flat map or piece of paper in equal proportions (see Fig. 2 on next page) so that when the torus is in final form, each color touches each one of the other six colors but never more than once. Once you have an actual colored torus as described above (see Figure 3), a line marking the seven color boundaries will unfold from the center in a vortex like manner as you rotate the torus

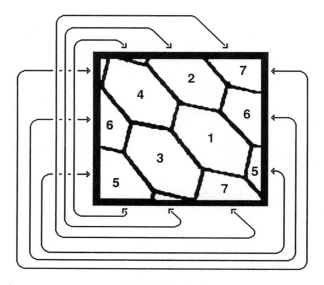

FIGURE 2

In the above seven color map, each color is of equal proportions and is represented by a number. When this square is connected by the various arrows and lines shown, it becomes a torus as illustrated in Figure 3. To produce this torus, or a rough approximation, connect the opposite edges of the square as shown by the lines and arrows. When the top and bottom are connected, the square becomes a cylinder. When the left and right edges are connected, the cylinder's ends are connected and the cylinder becomes a torus.

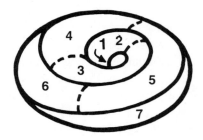

FIGURE 3

This torus showing a seven color map is redrawn after the style of Arthur Young in "The Reflexive Universe" Copyright © by Arthur Young.

F I G U R E   4

The above illustration is a two-dimensional rendition of the "vortex"
or "line" that manifests when the seven color torus is rotated
in upon itself. From twenty-seven different angles, all twenty-seven
letters of the Hebrew alphabet will appear.
Copyright © 1993 by Stan Tenen

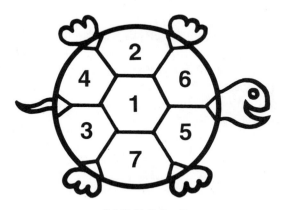

F I G U R E   5

Note how the pattern on a turtle's back fits the same pattern of the
square seven color map in Figure 2. The turtle's is a natural
representation of a torus in two dimensional form.
Copyright © 1993 by Stan Tenen

through itself. If this concept is difficult, imagine the torus having a skin of seven colors. As you push the blue part of the skin towards the center, all of the other colors of the skin will move accordingly. The lines of the boundaries will fold into the center of the torus tracing out a vortex shape (see Figure 4). Again, you can observe all twenty-seven letters of the Hebrew alphabet by observing this vortex from different angles.

Of particular significance regarding this discovery is that the seven colored torus laid out in two dimensional form gives the appearance of a turtle (see Figure 5).* This is further backed up by the fact that a turtle shell reveals the same hexagonal pattern.

What all of this proves is that not only is there an inherent orderliness in the universe, but that it is reflected in languages and native mythologies. There is a connection to the divine that has been lost. It was this ordered mental and language structure that enabled the ancient Babylonians to thrive both spiritually and physically. After the desolation of the Tower of Babylon, the ancients lost their ability to speak the divine tongue and were fated not to understand each other. Society accordingly degenerated.

All of this information tells us what any honest archeologist has already learned: the ancients knew more than we do today. Exactly what they knew and the nature thereof will be examined in the rest of this book. That the revelation comes through a location known as Turtle Cove at Montauk Point should not be forgotten.

---

* The word turtle derives from tortoise which means tortus (twisted). Webster's New World Dictionary gives a hypoethetic derivation of the Latin *tortus* as being derived from Late Greek tartarouchos, evil demon, originally controlling Tartarus.

TURTLE COVE

This is Turtle Cove facing west. If one enters the Camp Hero section of
Montauk Point State Park from the southeast gate (also known as
the fishermen's entrance) and travels to the fishing area, one will find
the remnants of a paved road that used to be Montauk Highway.
A short walk down that road and amidst the rushes,
there is a small path that leads to Turtle Cove.

Want to learn about other dimensions?

What you have just read in this chapter is a brief introduction to the Meru Foundation (a non-profit organization) and the work of Stan Tenon. You are encouraged to pursue this information by writing to the following address:

The Meru Foundation
PO Box 1738
San Anselmo, California 94979

Many tapes and models are available which will explain the information given here is more elaborate detail. It is an intriguing study which will enhance your ability to understand how other dimensions can exist in respect to the geometry of space and time. It is all highly recommended.

11

MONTAUK AND THE GRID

What you have read in the last chapter has been considered privileged information for centuries, yet it was always available to anyone who asked the right questions. It is all common sense when you think about it. Although Montauk and its history has been a major mystery to the general populace, its position as a gateway situated on the morphogenetic grid has been no secret to the various mystery schools. This explains not only the journey of Thomas Jefferson to retrieve the language of the Montauks but the locale's fascination to the Germans and its use during the Montauk Project.

Montauk is, of course, not the only such gateway but is receiving considerable attention because of what has occurred there. The negative activities and programming that occurred during the Montauk Project have been aptly described as crimes against humanity. They could also be described as crimes against the grid. If we are going to heal the rift that has occurred at Montauk, we are going to have to start by unveiling the mysteries surrounding it. This has begun in part with the books that have been written up to this point, but it also includes the curriculum of the mystery schools that orchestrated the endeavor in the first place. We cannot blame the United States Government whose officials are only on the surface of any possible conspiracies.

We cannot expect to cover the entire agenda and learning

systems of the various mystery schools on Earth. That is a gargantuan task. But, we can begin to cover some of the pertinent and basic points. The information on the function of the morphogenetic grid was the beginning. Next, we will examine how the structure of the morphogenetic grid takes place through the evolution of the Platonic solids (see illustration). Named after Plato, who studied them, the Platonic solids are the five basic shapes of solid geometry: the tetrahedron, cube, octahedron, icosahedron and dodecahedron. The evolutionary processes of these geometric shapes has long been guarded information and is very basic to understanding universal evolution. It was touched upon in the last chapter and will be examined a little more in depth right now in order that you understand the most basic concept of evolution.

In order that you understand the first concept of a grid, consider the simple example of a ship's navigator. When an ocean going vessel is at sea, the navigator has to keep a consistent eye on the bearings. The bearings refer to the position of a ship with regard to other fixed points such as rocks, mountains or buoys. The navigator uses a compass balanced by a gyroscope in order to determine his position in space. If there are no rocks or other points of dead reckoning, he also uses a sextant and various celestial bodies that can be found in the heavens. The whole idea is for him to reference himself with regards to space. The lines of latitude and longitude he employs from maps are an invaluable tool although they are an arbitrary system.

A navigator is simply trying to find out where his ship is located in terms of space and time. When we consider the morphogenetic grid of the Earth, we are still dealing with the idea of a referential system but are also taking on the idea of consciousness. Each and every living organism has to reference itself in space and time in order to survive. The whole idea of honoring one's father and mother is basically acknowledging where one came from. It is a reference point in the stream of time and space. Of course, there are many other such reference points.

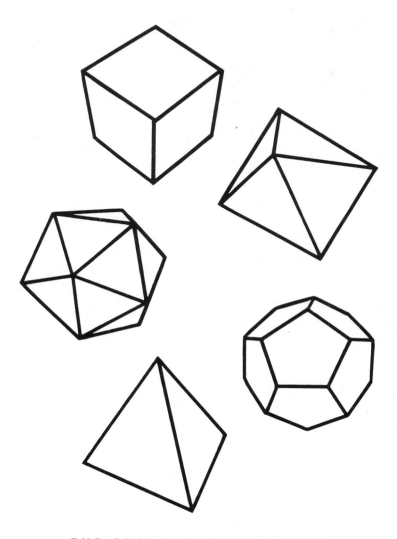

THE FIVE PLATONIC SOLIDS
Above clockwise from upper right are the octahedron, dodecahedron,
tetrahedron, icosahedron and cube. These shapes are all
referential to each other in that any of them can
be arrived at by utilizing the tetrahedron
as the basic shape.

If we want to survive, it becomes vital to reference ourselves as dutifully as is humanly possible. This includes the comprehension of the entire universe and our own position with regard to it. Native American shamans understand this in a rudimentary sense at the very least. They teach that there are six directions: north, south, east, west, above and below. These directions form the basis of a three dimensional grid.

If one then extends outward along any one of the six directions, it stands to reason that he or she will eventually stop somewhere along that grid and an arbitrary point will be fixed at that position. If one then scribes a sphere that is equidistant from the center to that fixed point, all directions will be accounted for. This is the first act of consciousness and it is sometimes represented as the orb of creation or the egg. Cabalists would refer to it as a Sephiroth which means sphere.

The second act of consciousness would be to duplicate the sphere just created. This creates a shape known as the vesica pisces which is illustrated below:

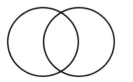

Point A

The vesica pisces is the football shaped object in the center which is formed as the result of two spheres intersecting. It has also been represented as a fish (it literally means fish bladder or fish vessel) and has been used as a symbol for Christ. The vesica pisces is said to contain all the wisdom in the universe, in part because all of creation can be derived from it. If you were to view the vesica pisces from the side (Point A), you will get another view which looks like a UFO (assuming the spheres are transparent and you are looking at a three dimensional representation). See the top of the next page.

90

The third act of creation would be a third sphere and the resultant glyph would be as follows:

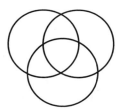

With very little imagination in two dimensions, one can see that an equilateral triangle can be formed by connecting various interstices. If you add another sphere and juxtapose them so that all are closely packed around a common center, a tetrahedron is created. The tetrahedron is very special because through means of duplicating itself it can in turn manifest into a cube, octahedron, icosahedron and dodecahedron. This is what is known as the unfolding of the Platonic solids.

The Platonic solids are defined as a series of exactly five shapes mathematically possible in three-dimensional geometry whose lines are of equal length and whose angles are of equal degree, thus creating plane surfaces of exactly the same shape and size. These five shapes are the same ones mentioned in the previous paragraph. Every shape in creation, biological or otherwise can be reduced to the pattern of one of these five Platonic solids.

Although the Platonic solids are named after Plato, he learned much of his information from the Pythagorean mystery school. Pythagoras taught all aspects of geometry with particular reference to how it relates to consciousness. The five Plantonic solids are vital to understanding the grid and all of human creation. Buckminster Fuller has even received academic acclaim by demonstrating that all of creation consists of tetrahedron shapes in one form or another. Fuller even patented his work on the grid and the Russians procured it for their own use. Unfortunately, Fuller's work is not written in such a fashion as to be easily understandable to the common man and has gone unnoticed by most people. But, his work is said to contain all the secrets of the universe. Some people may be familiar with his patented geodesic dome which is the most visible edifice at Disney's EPCOT Center in Florida. It is composed entirely of tetrahedrons.

The entire process of creation and evolution can be viewed as an unfoldment of geometry but also an unfoldment of consciousness because it was consciousness that made the first movement in space. As the reflection of self occurs in consciousness, one tries to reference oneself in space and time and the six cardinal directions become apparent. All of this is a simple overview of what is a very deep subject. One can get an even better understanding by creating the various Platonic solids with styrofoam balls and sticks and seeing how they unfold. Stan Tenon's tapes will help immeasurably in this regard. If one wants to take it a step further, one can study the work of Buckminster Fuller which is available in most libraries.

Despite all the logic offered for a grid, one can still ask another question: how did it all happen in the first place? Or, was it a big bang?

As is stated in many different philosophies and religions, before the beginning there was a void. In that void existed the potential for all things. Once the first act of consciousness was performed, that was it. Every conceivable geometric connection that could be made was made and the entire projection of creation occurred. We are somewhere along in the process of that right now.

It was along these geometric principles that the energy grid of the Earth was formed. A matrix of lines defined by shape, the energy grid of our planet is determined by the un-

92

foldment of the Platonic solids. As these solid lines of energy intersect and interact with one another, various mechanics occur. For example, when two lines of energy intersect at a cross point, a node is created. Nodes are standing waves that result in upwellings and inwellings of energy. An inwelling might result in a canyon, a deep hole or even a whirlpool like Charybdis (an actual whirling vortex of water near Italy that sucked in many sailors in Greek mythology). Upwellings might take the form of volcanoes, mountain ranges or geysers.

Inwellings and upwellings often appear together and are created by the mutual reinforcement of each other. For example, you might find huge caves within a big mountain. Men-an-Tol in Cornwall, England is an example of an inwelling of energy as it contains a hole but there is also a perfectly shaped phallic rock immediately astride it which is an upwelling. Montauk has always been described as a mountain, yet it contains a bottomless lake and a huge conical spire off the coast that once wrecked the hull of a ship called the *Great Eastern* in 1862. There are also huge caverns underground.

These precise locations of upwellings and inwellings have been mapped and zoned for the creation of artificial structures. They include the many pyramid complexes, the great stone circles such as Stonehenge, or the enhancement of natural structures thus creating what is known as sacred sites or Sacred Ground.

It is no accident that many of these same locales are often chosen for burial mounds. The reason is that bones contain the crystalline structure of the entity who used them and this establishes a link to the being's life information that has been stored within the energy grid. This permits communication with the dead and gives reason to protect the site, also allowing superstitious fear to keep such places hallow.

Montauk itself is full of the old bones of the Indians, particularly around the Montauk Manor. I have heard stories of workers ceasing to work on a condominium complex in the area because of hauntings. It was abandoned and never completed. Of course, the Montauk locals have aggravated the situation with the Indian spirits to no end. Decades ago, they had the audacity to build the Montauk Community Church with stones that were taken from the sacred Indian burial grounds. The church still stands today, stones and all. If you are brave, you can even attend its services on every Sunday. Just hope that it doesn't cave in.

At a cross point such as Montauk, energy can be tapped or used to inject or transfuse into the circulatory system of the planet. A person such as Duncan Cameron became a vital link to such an end. With extensive psychic training and esoteric technology, he would tap into "the heartbeat" of Mother Earth. He would become conversant with the various energies along the grid and could extract or feed information into it, depending on how he was being directed. Thoughts could be programmed to the masses or even the entire consciousness of time could be influenced.

Duncan was not chosen to do this work by accident. We have already witnessed remarkable synchronicity with the name Cameron. As will be told a little later in this book, I discovered that his person and his physical vehicle are tied to the grid in a manner that is nothing short of breathtaking.

12

THE MYSTERY SCHOOLS

The subject of who influences the Morphogenetic Grid is known as the science of Morphic Energy which has been the province and heritage of the "Ancient Wisdom and Mystery Schools". Protected and encrypted in the symbolism of Sacred Geometry, this knowledge has been reserved for the "Awakened" or "Initiated".

As these schools have always been dedicated to the study of consciousness and the nature of reality, it is their duty to make known the unknown and to pioneer and communicate other states of reality. Integrating the knowledge thus learned and turning it into an evolutionary educational program is an equally important part of their functions.

All of this would be fine except for one fact. Throughout history, the mystery schools have deviated into polarized groups at odds with each other in order to control the process of evolution. This has given rise to many different belief systems and religious constructs responsible for the guidance of moral conduct. The resulting conflict has generated war and indifference.

In such a context, belief systems are created with powerful events such as visions of the Virgin Mary, the resurrection and ascension of Christ, or visions of prophecy. Without even analyzing the exact nature of these miraculous occurrences, it is obvious that an incredible amount of dogma has been generated concerning them. What these miracles or prophecies imply for the future are substantiated only by faith with explicit doctrines designed to maintain them in our civilizations. People are not encouraged to discover and learn the truth but only to believe. "Good Deed Doers", swept away by their own convictions of faith, solicit others and whole generations are born into illusions of reality with fear and control buttons efficiently installed. Finally, prophecies are created to herd the many into subscribing to a particular creation of reality whatever it may be.

As there are many different mystery schools and religions, the number of people subscribing to each belief system or particular prophecy will have much to do with engineering the final outcome in the future. This is largely influenced by the power of thought feeding the grid. In such a manner, the greatest numbers that have invested into a prophecy will often prevail.

Based upon the above information, it should be clear that we are entirely capable of feeding the grid and determining the course of our own destiny. Therefore, evolution is in our own hands and our task becomes to take back that which we have lost. How do we do that? First, by opening what doors are available to us. That is how I acquired the information that is in this book. You will find your own doors as well.

13

THE MORPHOGENETIC GRID

That Turtle Cove is the legendary source of the universe is very representative of the idea that Montauk is a conduit or gateway to the vortex of creation itself. The inherent symmetry of the Hebrew alphabet was brought to your attention not because I want to convert you to Judaism but to demonstrate beyond a doubt that the process of creation was imprinted in the minds and souls of the ancients. The Sanskrit, Greek and Arabic alphabets also possess such divine symmetry and there are probably many other ancient languages that do the same.

The only reason *The Montauk Project* has been successful as a book is because the events it attempts to describe are considered remarkable and excite interest. The entire thesis of the book is that mankind can generate consciousness in such a manner as to manipulate matter, energy, space and time. At Montauk, the processes of creation were harnessed, at least for a short time. The only reason this is noteworthy or interesting is because the consciousness of society has divorced itself from the processes of creation. If everyone could do it, no one would be interested! Of course, this implies that there is a secret power in the universe who can accomplish such miracles and act as a hidden influence. This brings us to the realm of what has been known in our society as God.

Since the beginning of history, people have had disagreement concerning God, what he looks like and whether or not

He exists. Any logical and intelligent person can easily recognize that the common denominator for what is usually described as God could be more enthusiastically described as the creative principle of existence. No one has to believe in a bearded man with white robes in order to witness a flower blossom or the birth of a baby. These are creational processes and are viewed without denial. It is only when we associate these processes with divine beings of particular characteristics that we are likely to get social strife and religious wars.

Disagreement concerning the nature of creation is the result of divisive and polarized schools of thought that has gone on for millennia. If you possessed the secret to creation and didn't want anyone else to know it, you would do well to unfurl diverse schools of thought among the population and thereby incite debate and fighting. If you can keep the people distracted, they will never suspect there are even any worthwhile secrets to pursue. Of course, keeping the pot boiling soon becomes a full time job and the entire scenario becomes rather complex, not unlike our present circumstances on Earth today.

In America, there has been much debate between Creationists and Evolutionists. At the risk of oversimplifying the matter, Creationists believe that God created man from mud in a supernatural fashion while evolutionists maintain that man evolved from the animal kingdom. Both of these theories have some truth in them; just enough to keep people interested and arguing. Neither embrace what could be termed the actual theory of creation and evolution.

So what is the theory?

In all matter and biological organisms there are both seen and unseen processes. We can observe some of these unseen processes by dissection and microscopic inspection but no matter how far we break it down, there will still be unseen processes at work. The microscope can only take us so far. If we rely on our extrasensory perception or alter our state of consciousness, we could dig deeper as we leave our microscope and would eventually come to an incredible world of geometrical patterns that are whirling, interacting and doing all sorts of symmetrical wonders. All of these various patterns can be broken down into the five Platonic solids as were discussed previously. The evolution and interactions of these various shapes (the tetrahedron, the cube, the octahedron, the icosahedron and the dodecahedron) is known as the science of Sacred Geometry and all the laws of the physical sciences reflect and conform with it.

Atoms, molecules, snowflakes and flowers all evolve with respect to exact geometric interplays that result in varying degrees of harmony. Mathematical progression is easily viewable in the Periodic Table of chemistry. The science of biology is reduced to geometric shapes and swirls (helixes of the DNA strands) that conform to or can be derived from the five Platonic solids. The entire mechanics of this are infinite and are not intended to be the subject of this book. What is important is to identify the functional process of evolution and the fact that it conforms to these various shapes.

There is a branch of biology called morphology which concerns itself with the form and structure of plants and animals. The man who coined the word "morphology" was J.W. von Goethe, a German occultist who taught Rudolf Steiner, a close friend of Aleister Crowley. When Goethe and Steiner used the term morphology, they were also referring to the study of the form and structure of the Earth. This is also an approved dictionary definition as well, thus the word itself suggests a relationship between the biological and strictly physical aspects of existence.

As life evolves, it moves in a myriad of ways through these geometric patterns. Before biological life evolved on this planet, the Earth itself had to evolve along these same lines. By the time the Earth found itself revolving around the sun, it had already taken its physical shape and characteristics based in part upon the various other bodies orbiting in the heavens, its own orbit and spin plus whatever other cosmic variables might have been included in the equation. There were also other internal processes at work within the Earth's core structure and much of this had to do with geometrical patterns interfacing with the wiles of chaos. Any extraterrestrial beings involved would be supplementary to and complementary of the natural forces I am talking about here. It was in this context that biological life evolved.

The word geometry itself means "to measure the Earth". As lichen and plankton began to evolve into higher forms of life, it utilized the four alchemical elements of fire (the sun), water, earth and air. The consciousness of primitive life would have been in tune with the natural geometric or grid patterns on an instinctual basis. These grid lines serve as pathways to and from the creational process known as life. As stated earlier in this work, we call these pathways and its entire ecostructure the Morphogenetic Grid, "morph" meaning change and "genetic" referring to the genesis or beginning.

The Morphogenetic Grid can be understood as the conduit through which changes and thus evolutionary programs are conducted. We routinely see reflections of this function in every day life even if it is in terms of mundane things like fashion and social attitudes. Many of the intangibles and sensitive feelings in life can be ascribed to the morphogenetic grid. Homing pigeons and migrating birds also use the grid to determine where they are going. Slang and the Hundredth Monkey effect find their way to different geographical locations through the morphogenetic grid. The Hundredth Monkey effect is based on the fact that if a certain percentage of the monkey population learns something, the function will automatically telepath to all similar monkeys on the planet, even those who are isolated on an island. The critical monkey who bridges the gap is referred to as the "Hundredth Monkey".

Although anyone with the slightest sensitivity and intelligence can readily perceive or discover that such a grid exists, there is a much more sobering fact to consider once we accept that it exists: there is no one ostensibly in charge of it! In other words, there is apparently no one who is monitoring and programming evolution in a positive and business like manner. At least, if they are, they're not making themselves very well known. Most people, particularly your television commentators, are just muddling along in time and reporting their version of "what happens".

In recent years, there has been much panic "pumped into the grid" as people have focused on environmental crises. Some want us to believe the Earth is in direct threat of extinction by reason of a "greenhouse effect" or other means. Others want us to think that environmentalists have their own corrupt and sinister agenda. All of us are a part of this group consciousness and I have brought the environment issue to view as you probably have strong emotional feelings about it one way or another. You can "feel the pulse of the grid" in this manner. In the environmental issue, multiple sides have various agendas for wanting you to believe different things. The main threat to anyone's personal or larger environment is lack of accurate information.

As primitive forms of life like lichen and algae evolved, they emitted different waves, frequencies and electromagnetic phenomena in an attempt to survive and intermix with different elements and life forms. Eventually, different species evolved, each sharing the same electromagnetic codes with their brethren. But, all the different life forms shared one thing in common: the basic electromagnetic codes which are recognized as life. The energy between the species and the grid is interchangeable with the grid acting as a computer storehouse of information. Ordinary observation of life and evolution tells us that life evolves according to a program that has reference to every creature that has lived on the Earth. For all practical purposes, the computer exists within the energy stream of the Morphogenetic Grid. An entire study could be done in terms of computer terminology and the grid. And perhaps we will see some new innovative software on this subject in the future (anyone doing work in this direction should remember that it was John von Neumann who invented the modern computer).

The highway of information along the grid was called the "Sleeping Collective Unconscious" by Carl Jung and many others. Because we are all plugged into the grid, this highway allows for direct communication to occur between species and it is in this respect that an "Awakened Telepath" can read your thoughts. It is in this manner that we may define the path of thought as being instantaneously received or transmitted. Thought is the amplified response or action of the various energy bodies that make up an individual. These energy bodies are termed the Vital (physical), Emotional, Astral, Mental and the Subtle Energy light bodies. They encompass the entire vehicle of the physical body. When thought occurs, it is first processed as a disturbance in the subtle fields. Eventually the emotional body imprints this as a visual image before it is brought to the gross level as language. This is why a telepath can read your thoughts even if the language is unknown.

As a species, we create a matrix of energy known as the "Human Wave Form" and are fed as one body by the "Sleeping Collective Unconscious". This is why people in different locations can adopt the same habits, patterns or speech. And, on a deeper level, it is the Morphogenetic Grid which feeds the "Sleeping Collective Unconscious".

All of this data brings us to a very interesting question. Who programs the evolutionary computer and who feeds the Morphogenetic Grid? Before we examine this, we will first take another look at one of the "diskettes" used to write the programs on: Duncan Cameron.

14

PHARAOHS OF SCOTLAND

When Duncan Cameron did his work in the Montauk Chair, he sat near an arbitrary meridian (as measured on normal Earth maps) that is 72° from the Prime Meridian in Greenwich, England. If you follow this meridian due south you will follow it down the Atlantic Ocean and over the sunken ruins of Atlantis which become clearly visible as you reach the Caribbean Islands. This particular meridian runs through the island of Hispaniola which has long been renowned for its voodoo culture and extends right through Machu Picchu, the holy city of the Incas.

Sitting north of Atlantis, Duncan's primary work was done within the confines of a Native American holy ground and in the general vicinity of the bones of the Montauk Pharoah family. The royal legacy of this family reaches too far back for us to trace with ordinary history but points straight to the south and the lost continent of Atlantis.

Duncan's job, at least in part, was to traffic with the energies along the grid that the ancient Pharoah family had long guarded. The wisdom of these ancients and their guardianship of the grid was potentially accessible via the conduit of their nearby bones. Duncan was a perfect passageway to the energy of the ancient Pharoahs because his own lineage traces back to the Pharoahs of Egypt who, according to Edgar Cayce and many others, appeared from Atlantis.

The story of how this all came to light begins with my initial discovery of the name "Duncan Cameron" in Aleister Crowley's autobiography, *The Confessions of Aleister Crowley*. On page 361, he mentions a Ludovic Cameron who is also known as "Duncombe" or "Duncan" and wants to revive the Celtic nations in an empire. On page 366, he is referring to "Duncan Cameron" again when he makes a reference to MacBeth and quotes a passage, "Wake Duncan with thy knocking? I would thou could'st".

We have to wonder if Shakespeare, who's work has been studied as a literal translation of the Cabala, was trying to wake up our Duncan Cameron. I didn't understand what significance this had at the time, but I figured intuitively that MacBeth would eventually find its way into the investigation of Duncan's family tree. Over two years later, I would receive a phone call from Jon Singer that would clarify the matter considerably. Out of the blue, Jon called and told me that he had been reading a book which indicated the real life MacBeth was descended from the Pharaohs of Egypt. His timing was excellent as I was wrapped up in a study of the Pharaohs at the time. The book was titled *MacBeth: High King of Scotland* by Peter Ellis.

According to information in this book, the Celts had originated in India and had migrated to Egypt under the leadership of Niul. He married the Pharaoh's daughter, Scota, who bore a son named Gaidheal Glas. The Pharaoh of this time was Chenthres who has also been identified as Ramses II (each Pharaoh was generally known to have at least five names). During the Passover persecution of the Jews, the Celts were forced to leave Egypt. They made their way to Palestine, North Africa and eventually to Spain and Ireland. When the Celts finally settled in the British Isles, they named their kingdom Scotland in honor of Scota, the Pharaoh's daughter. These Scots were obviously quite proud of their legacy that connected them to the Pharaoh.

There is further evidence to suggest that MacBeth was linked to the Pharaohs. The name "Beth" is derived from the Hebrew "bet" which is the first letter of their alphabet and is equivalent to our "b". It also means house from which the word "pharaoh" is also derived. As the first letter in the Hebrew alphabet, bet is also used to symbolize the vortex figure given in Chapter 10. The "Mac" in MacBeth signifies the family clan of "Beth".

If MacBeth was connected to the Pharaohs of Egypt, I decided I had better have a look at Shakespeare's play which I had never read or seen dramatized up to that point. The first character I encountered was King Duncan. As I continued to read what literature was readily available about *MacBeth*, I soon learned that Shakespeare had written a fictional and dramatic account of the slaying of an actual King Duncan by a general named MacBeth.

In what is arguably Shakespeare's greatest work, *MacBeth* was very much written for King James I of Scotland who was considered an expert on witchcraft. The historical figures MacBeth and King Duncan were first cousins who were both influenced by the witches of the day. The homeland of the witches was the Isle of Skye.

King Duncan was historically so merciful that he would not punish people. His loving kindness was taken advantage of and robbers sprung up with much societal chaos resulting. MacBeth was Duncan's general. He was effective and quick with the sword. When a Viking fleet from Norway attacked Scotland and had Duncan cornered, the king got a secret message to MacBeth who came to the rescue and did a remarkable job of defeating the Vikings and kicking them out of Scotland. Seeing his own potential for power and being under the influence of certain witches, MacBeth slew his cousin and took over the kingdom. He was an adept ruler and considerably calmed down the crime that had been prevalent under Duncan's reign. Unfortunately, MacBeth suffered the fate of many tyrants. He could trust no one and no one could trust him.

As soon as I shared this information with Preston Nichols, he immediately fired back that King Duncan's actual name was Alexander Duncan Cameron. Long before he ever met Duncan, this information was told to him by one of his high school English teachers who happened to be an expert on Shakespeare. I have as yet been unable to verify this historically but the names of King Duncan and his family are identical to those which are found in the Cameron Clan's family tree.

All of this study points directly to the Pharaonic heritage of the Scots (in the personage of Duncan Cameron) meeting the Pharaonic heritage of the Native Montauks at the grand central crossroads of time known as Montauk Point.

Of course, plenty of mistakes were made. If not, you wouldn't be sitting at the perimeter of reality reading this book. Duncan's own genetic vehicle was harnessed and misused. In turn, he was used to access the grid and the knowledge and energy of the ancients. It appears that nothing but confusion and disaster resulted from the abuse of the Pharaonic energy. It is therefore no coincidence that the biggest missing ingredient in today's culture is the role of the Pharaoh. We will explore that in the next chapter.

15

THE PHARAOH
AND ANCIENT WISDOM

In ancient times, it was the Pharaoh who stood as guardian of the ancient wisdom that trafficked across the grid. In Egypt, the Pharaoh was defined as that which unites the upper and lower Nile. This description was intended to be symbolic of where the upper and lower triangles are united as visualized in the Seal of Solomon (more popularly recognized as the Star of David). The upper triangle, pointing upwards, symbolizes the higher energies and the esoteric world. The lower triangle, pointing downwards, represents the exoteric world which includes outward manifestation and all mundane matters of the Earth. The concept of a Pharaoh is an aware entity that works with the energies from the lower windows while still looking into the higher windows for direction and guidance. Without saying, the role of the Pharaoh is sadly lacking in the consciousness of today's society.

As the Pharaoh had access to both worlds, his duty was to interpret what information was deemed necessary to release to the outer world of society in order that evolution might achieve its divine manifestation. Ideally, the Pharaoh would balance the esoteric with the exoteric. In other words, he was pumping the morphogenetic grid with information. If a Pharaoh stood his ground and ruled wisely, society would evolve towards a paradise.

In addition to the Pharaoh's function, the mystery schools served their own ends and were involved in countless schemes. Whatever their specific agendas might be, all wanted the ear and access of the Pharaoh for it was there that the symbolic struggle for evolution was at its acme. This struggle included the battles of good versus evil which many philosophers have credited for making possible the evolutionary process. Because evil cannot be denied or eliminated, it must be balanced and it is at this point that the mystery schools come into play. Balancing of evil is essential to the constructs of the universe.

The Pharaonic line had its most severe setback at the time of Moses, an Egyptian high priest who was groomed for the Pharaohship. Moses literally initiated the downfall of Egypt by orchestrating the Exodus and taking off with the Arcadian staff, a magical/technical device handed down from Atlantis. For Moses to abandon his Egyptian divinity was devastating to the priesthood for his particular school was the last one to have been initiated in magic. Since that time period, the role of the Pharaoh has been compartmented and factionalized into various secret societies which vie for power and influence. The traditional role of the Pharaoh has been lost to the populace at large and the degradation of this institution is clearly dramatized in recent times by the plight of the Montauk Indians.

The word Pharaoh itself means "Great House". If you break down the etymology (which is the study of word origins) even further, you discover that the word "great" is derived from the Greek and Persian words (magos and maz respectively) for magic. "House" is derived from Indo-European word "skeu" or "keu" which means "to hide". Translated, this all means that the word Pharaoh means "magic hiding place". It fits the description of this puzzle perfectly.

While the Pharaoh represented the magic hiding place in human form, the actual physical representation of magic was the Great Pyramid. This pyramid is shaped like the top half of an octahedron. Still unknown to many, there is a reverse pyramid constructed exactly beneath the base of the Great Pyramid. The top pyramid is known as the ante chamber and

108

represents creation while the reverse pyramid is known as the anti chamber and represents destruction. This makes for a black hole/white hole effect. Together, these two pyramids make an octahedron which is the exact shape of the Delta-T antenna described in *The Montauk Project*. The octahedron is a very key shape in the structure of the Earth's grid. If you can imagine two interlocking tetrahedrons within the structure of the Earth itself, an octahedron would be nestled in the center in a continuous rotation. By generating waves through the field of this octet shape, one can change space and time itself.

If one considers that the Earth contains geometric grid patterns that are in continuous rotation, one can grasp that the octahedron would likewise rotate. One must remember that particles in space and time are not continuous. They appear and reappear but our perception is in synch (like watching a movie) so that these particles appear to be solid and never moving. The particles themselves are created by electromagnetic pulsations that use the octahedron as a conduit.

One can get a rough idea by constructing a small octahedron and considering that it is within its own reference frame and within the confines of its own dimension. Now, rotate it 90° at a time on its lateral axis and count the number of points that could receive a pulsation. You will find twelve before you return it to its original position. If one counter rotates the octahedron, there will be another twelve points which makes a total of twenty-four potential realities. If one then rotates and counter rotates the octahedron on its vertical axis, the number of realities will come to 48.

Each rotation of the original octahedron made up twelve different realities. It is important to note the number "twelve" because it is a sacred number. It is reflected in the twelve months of the year, twelve signs of the zodiac, twelve disciples of Christ and various other ways. The most basic example of twelve as a sacred number is if we take a sphere, like a marble, and pack as many spheres as possible around it. You will find that twelve spheres or marbles fit exactly around the one. Of course, this suggests that thirteen is also a sacred number. We all know there has been much supersition surrounding it. There are thirteen members in a witches coven, thirteen people at the Last Supper if you include Christ and thirteen months in the lunar calendar. The number thirteen is also a prime number and was sacred to the ancients.

In the above example, we demonstrated twelve different realities around a central reference point. The entire example is an oversimplification of the entire procedure but will serve to give a very general idea on how geometry interfaces with different realities.

As one begins to study the symmetry of reality, it becomes easy to grasp that magical arts were based on definite geometrical principles. Unfortunately, you will find it next to impossible to find a witch or astrologer who fully understand these principles yet their whole reason for being is based upon them! The knowledge, as stated elsewhere, was taken away and hidden.

What we call the Great Pyramid at Giza was essentially the top half of an octahedron which was built to mimic the Earth's grid so as to affect a potential interface with other realities. Another curious fact about the Great Pyramid is that within its walls almost every possible description of Egyptian life was given except for who built the pyramid and why. If the builders were so emphatic about explaining such mundane aspects as how Egyptians wash, you would assume that they would have also described how they built the pyramid and what their reasons were. This was secret and was not meant to be shared with anyone but those initiated in the mystery schools. If you understand the working principles of the octahedron as described above, you have come a long way towards understanding what the Great Pyramid was all about.

When you consider the above realities alluded to in the above example, you begin to realize that the morphogenetic grid itself parlays itself into many different realities and is not exclusive to our own particular "Earth reality". The pyramid was a way station or a threshold to these other worlds and to the information on the grid itself.

In summary, the pyramid was the magic hiding place and

the Pharaoh was the personal representative of that secret. As any knowledge represents potential power, it was his job to stand as guardian so as to maintain a balance between the higher and lower worlds. Of course, the Pharaoh was in human form. There was actually another character with a far more important role in the course of evolution and he lived in the Great Pyramid itself.

16

TAHUTI

Sometimes known as the Dweller on the Threshold, Tahuti was a key figure in the Egyptian pantheon and was said actually to reside in the Great Pyramid. Usually portrayed as an Ibis, if not a dog or an ape, Tahuti was the god of wisdom, learning and magic. Also the inventor of numbers, Tahuti is best known as the scribe of the gods. The Greeks referred to him as Thoth, but also identified him as Hermes. The Romans called him Mercury and the Hebrews knew him as Enoch.

More to our immediate interest, Tahuti not only resided in the Great Pyramid, he was the builder of it. Of course, none of this means that he actually carried stones or stood over the workers as a foreman with a hard hat. As scribe of the gods, Tahuti absorbed all available knowledge and "wrote programs" (to use the computer analogy) in accordance with the various factors of evolution. He acted as a filter of all the various information that came in off the morphogenetic grid and, to use computer terms again, he would be better described as a systems analyst.

The function of Tahuti and his role in creation itself digs much deeper.

If you read the Gospel according to St. John, it will say "In the beginning was the Word and the Word was God". "The Word" is meant to mean Logos or the divine principle or character of existence. Etymologically, "word" means verb. In

113

other words, the first action in the universe was a verb or activity of some sort. We can call it the First Cause or whatever we want.

The First Cause was for something to emerge from nothing or no-thing. This soon results in a sphere as was described in an earlier chapter and a tetrahedron unfolds a few steps later. As the god of numbers and geometry, Tahuti is credited with the creation of the tetrahedron and thus the pyramid. He built the Great Pyramid so that it would have a resonance with the grid of the Earth and thereby create a dwelling place for himself. His role was to serve as a bridge between this dimension and the other worlds.

As the god of numbers, Tahuti was not only involved in the creation process, his writings recorded the process and the knowledge that went with it. Throughout history, this information has been primarily relegated to the various secret societies of civilization.

One of Tahuti's greatest secrets was known as the process of Tetragrammaton which you may already be familiar with. It is found in the Bible and in the dictionary but a complete understanding of the term is deliberately obscured. Books on witchcraft and secret societies will sometimes teach a portion of Tetragrammaton and say that it is highly secretive and not to be spoken of and will be learned after a long process of initiation. Much mumbo jumbo has arisen over the use of the word.

If you look in the dictionary, Tetragrammaton is merely defined as the four consonants of the Hebrew name for God. Depending on the translation, it is either JHVH, YHVH or YHWH. When vowels are added it becomes Yahweh or Jehovah which will be readily recognizable to most people. Few clergymen, if any, really understand what this concept means.

Aleister Crowley recognized the above definition and readily added that the four letters Yod, Hé, Vau, and Hé correspond to the four elements of fire, water, air, and earth. He also explains that the four letters are symbolic of the father or first principle who in turn begets the mother who is the female or negative principle. Their union brings together the son who is their heir. A twin daughter is also produced who is the end product. It is the father's role to make the daughter his bride so that she can take over for her mother. Then, the daughter embraces the father and thereby rekindles the powers of the primordial All-Father. This is presented not as a rite of incest but as a magical principle which is at the heart of all creation. Crowley has more to say but he does not spill all the beans. There are, of course, myriad ways to look at this formula and to conjure with it.

Although it might already be in print in some obscure fashion, the big secret about Tetragrammaton has to do with its etymology. The first five letters of the word spell "tetra" which means four. In other words, here is the tetrahedron surfacing again. Additionally, "tetra" as a phoneme can be traced back to "tort" which means to twist or rotate. This brings to mind the idea of the tetrahedron rotating as a creational process. The meaning of "grammaton" refers to something written, specifically letters. This brings us back to the work of Stan Tenon and the fact that Hebrew letters are formed from "fire" within the tetrahedron. Of course, the four letters of Tetragrammaton are Yod, Hé, Vau, and Hé. Many occultists know this, but they do not link it to the tetrahedon, the four points of which correspond to fire, water, earth and air. And, if they do understand the principle, they certainly don't say too much about it.

The idea that the tetrahedron is the basic genesis of life cannot be overstated enough and that is at least one reason why I have taken the opportunity to give different views of this principle. As was stated earlier, all shapes can be derived from the tetrahedron. In a process known as Tet-tracking, whereby tetrahedrons are juxtaposed in whatever form is desirable, almost any shape in creation can be manifested. The DNA spiral, which is the very seed of life itself, can be easily derived through Tet-tracking. If you stack thirty-three (a master number in numerology) tetrahedrons face to face, it will form a spiral or helix shape. If you splice this spiral of thirty-three tetrahedrons in half, it will form two helixes which duplicates the form of DNA exactly (DNA consists of two helixes). Once this done, the number of solid geometric faces on the two helixes is 66.666. This is why Crowley and others have called 666 the number of man. It is encoded in our DNA.

This is also an opportune time to point out that there is another key correspondence to 666 in the periodic table of chemistry. This has to do with carbon which is known as element number twelve. All life on this planet is considered to be carbon based because the carbon atom is conspicuously present in all living things. Carbon has six electrons, six protons and six neutrons. Again, we have 666.

Crowley was not only keenly aware of the significance of 666, he was a patron of Tahuti and dedicated most of his last years to finishing one of his better books which is entitled *The Book of Thoth.* This is one of the most authoritative books on the Tarot. The word "Tarot" is also spelled TARO which also sheds some interesting light. Occultists say that TARO derives from ROTA which means wheel. ROTA is also the root of the word "rotation". Regular etymology also traces the word "Tarot" back to tort which again means tortus or twist. Not only does the tetrahedron continue to surface as we study sacred information but so does the idea of rotation which is of equal importance. If you refer back to the previous chapter, rotation of the octahedron shape was demonstrated as to how reality manifests through various dimensions.

If Crowley has left his mark on Montauk, it could be said that Tahuti has too. The Ordo Templi Orientis or OTO has a Tahuti Lodge which meets out at Montauk. Further, the head of the OTO once informed me that he edited Jack Parsons' book *Freedom Is a Two-Edged Sword* while visiting his Montauk brethren. At this point, we can safely say that correspondences of this nature are endless.

In summary, Tahuti is a god (or a creative function of the universe) who is the repository of all sacred information. He was there in the beginning and has acted as the god of learning ever since. The knowledge possessed by Tahuti can be accessed by anyone willing to take the initiative required. As he dwells in the pyramid, or the way station to the fourth dimension, he can offer a pathway out of this realm. Unfortunately, throughout history this pathway has been either blocked, abandoned or closely guarded by the various mystery schools and priesthoods. A veil was thus established that was virtually impossible to penetrate except by the most adept students of the universe. Of course, this has everything to do with the principle of the survival of the fittest and the consequent death of those who are not able to adapt.

In the previous chapter, it was said that the Pharaoh would look into the upper windows while interfacing with the lower windows of existence. When an ancient Pharaoh penetrated the upper windows, he could be said to be "going beyond the veil" and immersing himself into the time gates of ancient wisdom. Few people in modern times have even been aware of the veil, let alone how to "pierce" it. It was only for the privileged few.

The mystery schools of ancient Egypt taught these very secrets. A few of these have already been given in this book, but some of their most ancient and protected wisdom had to do with one of the earlier correspondences we encountered in this book: the planet Mars. That the name of their ancient city, Al-Khahira or Cairo, means Mars should not go unheeded. In the next chapter, we shall examine some of the ancient history of the red planet.

17

A HISTORY OF MARS

The planet Mars has stood out on the horizon of man's consciousness more so than any other celestial body with the possible exceptions of the moon and the sun. Venus is closer and shines brighter in the twilight hours but Mars gets most of the attention. We will accordingly explore just why it is that the red planet is so deeply rooted within the consciousness of mankind.

Probably the most classic example of Mars' effect on the psyche of man was the *War of the Worlds* broadcast by Orson Welles on Halloween in 1938. People all across New Jersey were running for the hills because they thought the Martians had landed. This was all despite the fact that the program had been announced as fiction. Why were people so quick to jump and not prudent enough to switch the radio dial or just call the different authorities?

If one goes back to the turn of the century and even later, one finds tremendous enthusiasm about life on Mars. The viewpoint of society and the scientific community was much less arrogant in those days and the various literature from the time period is fascinating reading from today's perspective.

One of the most interesting characters from this era was Percival Lowell, a famous astronomer and scientist who built an observatory at Flagstaff, Arizona for the exclusive purpose of observing Mars. He observed canals and was convinced that they possessed water at one point in history. His claims that Mars was inhabited by beings capable of building a planet wide irrigation system were disputed and his pro-life views on the planet Mars were often ridiculed. Lowell is similar to Tesla in that he was a reputed scientist yet made claims that were considered taboo to conventional scientists. Lowell's calculations were quite precise in astronomy and led to tracking down the planet Pluto which was discovered in the 1930s. As a distinguished scientist, his other claims bear closer inspection. During his life, no one possessed a more powerful telescope than Lowell but many were too quick to counter his views. One of his strongest opponents was Alfred Wallace who helped pioneer the "Theory of Evolution". While that might say enough in itself, Wallace claimed the Martian temperature was too low and that no water could inhabit the planet. He further said that Mars was "absolutely UNINHABITABLE!".

Arthur C. Clarke has stated that Lowell was one of the most fascinating characters in the history of astronomy. Although Clarke claims that Lowell's canals are now proven not to exist (there are some scientists who would dispute that), he makes a telling statement:

"Now that we have good quality photographs of Mars, someone should compare Lowell's drawings with the reality to try and find just what happened up there at Flagstaff at the turn of the century. How was it possible for a man to sustain a self-consistent and extremely detailed optical illusion (if that *is* what it was) over a period of more than twenty years? How did he convince others of his vision? What correlation, if any, was there between the ability of other astronomers to see the canals, and their position on the Lowell Observatory payroll? These are just a few questions that might be asked..."

Obviously, Clarke is assuming that the photographs and data relayed to him (proving the canals don't exist) were correct. NASA has a reputation for giving out compartmentalized photographs. Although Clarke seems quite ready to implicate Lowell's staff, he at least acknowledges a major anomaly in the history of Percival Lowell.

If we look a bit deeper into the Martian scenario, we find that there were huge magnetic storms on the planet in 1903 that ranged from May to August. On August 13, these storms appeared in pictures in "Science News" magazine. Serious theories have been offered to suggest that these magnetic storms were creating an atmosphere so as to set up civilization once again. A meltdown of the ice cap and extensive cloud cover provided moisture, oxygen and all the components that would be conducive to organic life. Lowell was one of the few people who witnessed it. Lowell's theories and claims about Martian life have been thoroughly discounted and "disproven" by modern scientific thought. If one believes all the data and conclusions offered by conventional science, there is at least one gaping and unscientific assumption on their part. They are assuming that the Mars viewed by Lowell is the same one they are viewing today. Any number of scenarios are possible. I have been flatly told by one person that Lowell was on the verge of discovering a major time travel experiment whereby our civilization was making Mars habitable.

When one examines all the available data (and there is plenty more I've yet to see*), it appears that Lowell's scientific observations may have led him into contact with aliens or humans from the future. It is also possible they were Martians. At the very least, it was the mystery schools who supplied him with information about strange anomalies in the solar system. This becomes believable if you consider that he knew information that was standard mystery school fodder. For example, he knew there was a gravitational effect on the planet Neptune before anyone else in regular society did. This eventually led to the discovery of Pluto by the scientific community after his death. He was also aware of the planet Vulcan. This is a small planet which orbits the sun inside of Mercury and its discovery

---

* I have not been able to locate any of Lowell's books at this writing, but I have spoken to a representative of the Lowell Observatory in Flagstaff. They've informed me that a review of the archives might be possible but there are no books available by mail order. One has to visit the gift shop in person. This will require a future trip someday.

has been a scandal that NASA and modern astronomers often refuse to admit. Lowell was also aware of another unusual piece of information and that is the fact that there is a third movement of the planets that is overlooked by most texts. We all know about orbital movements and ordinary planetary rotation, but there is also a very slow north/south rotation of the planets. This will take a long time to accomplish but will eventually result in the planets of our solar system being upside down so that the sun rises in the west and sets in the east. This is already the case with Uranus and Neptune.

Lowell's insights into this type of information indicate that he was on some path of initiation. It certainly made him out of bounds for serious media coverage. Although he died a sudden death in 1916 (if we believe the popular press), he left a serious legacy behind.

Even though Lowell was dead, there was still much enthusiasm in the popular press that life might exist on the red planet. Consciousness of Mars was so strong in 1924 that the Chief of Naval Operation and the Director of the U.S. Army Signal Corps sent dispatches to their stations to maintain radio silence while Mars was at its closest opposition (to Earth) of this century. The *New York Times* even reported strange radio signals that came through from the planet that didn't make any ordinary sense except that they revealed a repeated pattern of a face! This article is reproduced on the opposite page. Later in the book, you will read a brief account of a time travel experiment that occurred in 1923. One has to wonder if there is a correspondence between that experiment, "Lowell's Mars" being wiped out, and the face on Mars being transmitted in 1924.

We have to ask ourselves why no one has looked deeper into these various contending viewpoints concerning the planet Mars. Most popular literature on this topic has been embarrassingly shallow. Most certainly, the information on the subject is not abundant and is deliberately obscured. We only have to look a bit earlier in history at Jules Verne's work to realize that something odd was at work. He wrote about the two moons of

SEEKS SIGN FROM MARS IN 30-FOOT RADIO FILM

Dr. Todd Will Study Photograph of Mysterious Dots and Dashes Recently Recorded.

WASHINGTON, Aug. 27.—The development of a photographic film record of radio signals during a period of about twenty-nine hours, while Mars was closest to the earth, has deepened the mystery of the dots and dashes reported heard at the same time by widely separated operators of powerful stations.

C. Francis Jenkins of Washington, inventor of the device, which he calls the "radio photo message continuous transmission machine," was induced by Dr. David Todd, professor emeritus of astronomy of Amherst and organizer of the international "listening-in" for signals from Mars, to take the record.

The film, thirty feet long and six inches wide, discloses in black on white a fairly regular arrangement of dots and dashes along one side, but on the other side at almost evenly spaced intervals are curiously jumbled groups each taking the form of a crudely drawn face.

"I don't think the results have anything to do with Mars," says Mr. Jenkins. "Quite likely the sounds recorded are the result of heterodyning or interference of radio signals. The film shows a repetition at intervals of about a half hour, of what appears to be a man's face. It's a freak which we can't explain."

The above article is a word for word reproduction of an article that appears on page 6 of the August 28, 1924 edition of the *New York Times*.

Mars before they were officially discovered in 1877 by Asaph Hall. In addition to talking to the top scientists of the day, Verne had extensive connections with various secret and mystical societies that included the Golden Dawn, OTO and Theosophical Society.

Looking earlier in history, we find that in 1726 Jonathan Swift mentioned the two moons of Mars in his classic book *Gulliver's Travels.* He even noted pertinent observations about their orbits and distance from their parent planet. The implication is that both of these writers were either members of secret societies or had access to ancient writings. The Greek poet Homer wrote about the two steeds of Mars which were named Phobos (fear) and Deimos (flight or rout or panic). These were the horses that pulled the chariot of the god Mars. When Asaph Hall discovered the two moons, several names were proposed and he unwittingly selected the names by which these heavenly bodies were known to the ancients. If one digs yet deeper, one finds a reservoir of information that includes ancient writings and scripture that gives a much different tint on Mars.

Ancient texts reveal that our entire perception of time has been deeply influenced by the planet Mars. The calendar itself was based upon the activity of the planet. This began when Biblical scribes noticed the regular fly-bys of Mars and dutifully recorded them. As the lives of these scribes were not long, they depended on the calendar and writings to evaluate an extended period of time. In those days, history was a different art form than that of today and was considered to be totally relevant to current conditions.

According to these ancient observations, there was a perfectly resonant orbit between Mars and Earth.* Mars took exactly 720 days to orbit the sun and the Earth took 360 days to accomplish the same feat. One learns in school that the ancients incorrectly estimated that a year was 360 days but that our modern scientific thinkers discovered that the Earth orbits

---

* Free energy is based upon this model of two orbiting bodies being in each others harmonic fields.

the sun once every 365.25 days. The ancients are always portrayed as being so dumb!

The scribes noted that the Ides of March (March 15th) and October 26th were the major fly-by dates of the two planet's orbits. Both of these dates became cardinal points on the calendar. The Ides of March marked the beginning of spring and the end of winter. The fly-by of Mars on October 26th marked the harvest and marked the end of the year for the ancient Celtics and other peoples.*

Another pattern that the ancient historians noted was that Mars came frighteningly close every 108 years. Some accounts even gave the impression Mars was so close that people could actually see what was going on. This included the observation of canals. The reason for this close observation of the planet Mars was, according to at least one source, a dome of water that covered the atmosphere of Earth. This resulted in a magnification of all heavenly bodies, particularly Mars which is a very close neighbor. As for the dome of water, it is said to have caused a deluge of water when the misuse of laser type weapons caused it to collapse.

Eventually, during one of these close fly-bys, a major cataclysm occurred when the gravitational pulls became too close for comfort. It is entirely possible that other factors may have been involved as well. These could have included the planet Venus or outside interference.

This cataclysm was described as a major event in the Bible. In the Battle of Beth-horun from the Book of Joshua, there is the Longest Day of Joshua where they did rituals in anticipation of the above moment. They marched around the wall every day until the Sabbath. On that day, they marched around seven times and history records this as the day the sun stood still. What happened was that the two planets almost

---

* March (which means Mars) was once the first month of the year. This fact is revealed in our Gregorian calendar which uses the following months: September, October, November and December. These mean 7, 8, 9 and 10 respectively. In other words, September is seven months away from March, October is eight, etc.

collided and a very major cataclysm took place on Mars. Earth was shaken up as well and the walls of Jericho came down.

What happened on the day the sun stood still was that the geometrical physics of the situation created a twenty-eight hour day. As a consequence, the Earth gained velocity (like an electron) and more energy that eventually added approximately 5.25 days to our orbit. The Martian orbit changed from 720 to approximately 686 1/2 days. The astrologers (all astronomers were known as astrologers then) of the day began to calculate changes and soon realized that the commonly known equinoxes and solstices were not in the same place. Because the Temple of Solomon and various temples were constructed to coincide with certain heavenly events (often displaying shadows or other curious phenomena), the temples had to be rebuilt as they were now approximately 6° off their previous position. Accordingly, the beginning of Spring moved March 15th to approximately March 21st. This period of renewal was marked by the goddess Ishtar, identified with Venus (as said earlier, the planet Venus was involved in this near collision according to some accounts). A pagan festival celebrated Ishtar at this time period and the very word Easter is derived from this goddess.

The zodiac itself begins with Aries, a homonym for Ares who was the Greek god of War. The Romans identified Ares as Mars. In astrology, the constellation Aries is, of course, ruled by the planet Mars. All of this information clearly demonstrates that our entire system of time has paid tribute to Mars as the primary force in the heavens.

When 5.25 days were added to October 26th, this gave us October 31st as the day upon which to celebrate the harvest. This day is presently celebrated in the United States as Allhallows Eve or Halloween. This time period was very important to the ancients and November 1st was celebrated as Samhain or New Year's Day by the Druids. Thus, Halloween is really a celebration of Mars. It was additionally intended to symbolize a transmigration of souls from Mars to the Earth.

This great cataclysm between Mars and the Earth had yet another influence on our perception of time. According to one calendar, this big event occurred in 1440 B.C. (stands for either Before the Common Era or Before Christ). Another puts it at 1404 B.C. Note that the difference in the two calendars constitutes thirty-six years. This is a key number because some traditions believe it symbolizes the life of Christ and that His life represents the outermost impact of human consciousness. Of course, some mystery schools propagate the idea that Christ lived to be thirty-three. This is not the important point, but what is significant is to show how mystery schools will go to the lengths of changing a calendar based upon an event such as the life of Christ. They are trying to manipulate our consciousness and in this particular case through the use of time.

In the year 701 or 731 B.C., another near fly-by occurred as documented by the scribes. They back tracked astronomically and realized this was a 108 year cycle. In other words, throughout history there had been a cataclysm every 108 years as Mars flew by. Earth changes were a matter of course. It was this history of disaster and terror that earned Mars its identification as the warrior planet. Virtually all civilizations have identified Mars as the warrior or fire planet.

According to occult sciences, the Earth is in a cradle orbit. This means that it is in an orbit that is conducive to and promotes life. In ancient history, Mars was previously in the cradle orbit and would have been the center of life in the solar system at that time. In time, Earth will fall out of the cradle orbit and Venus will inherit it. All of the above is based upon the fact that the solar system itself is modeled after the structure of the atom and will eventually collapse in on itself. In such a scenario, life has to either ascend or to transmutate periodically if it wants to escape extinction. It is for this reason that Mars has left a deep scar in the psyche of Earthlings. We were once invaded and colonized.

In about the 16th or 17th century, New Year's Day was moved to January 1st. The idea was to move consciousness away from Mars and the worship of Baal. Many will remember Baal as the golden calf or fertility god from the movie *The Ten Commandments*. Baal was also an ancient city located just north of Cairo and is more popularly known as Heliopolis by historians. It reached extensively throughout the Mideast. As was Cairo named after Mars, the culture of Baal was Martian. The gospels have St. Paul shrewdly blasting the worship of Baal on the Hill of Mars. The story of Moses in the Old Testament shows him to be breaking away from the Baal or Martian tradition, but it is interesting to note that the founder of Hasidism (a very influential sect of Jewish mystics who are well known in New York) was born Israel ben Eliezer but chose his name to be Baal Shem Tov. Perhaps he was reading between the lines or had access to information that is not popularly passed around in synagogues.

There is an interesting genetic substantiation of the idea that life actually transmigrated from Mars to Earth. The blood lineage that emerged from the locality of ancient Baal turns out to be the same as that of the Gaelic races that settled in the Pyrenees and St. Angeles, Italy. Sixty to ninety percent of these people have Rh negative blood. Although most people have heard of the term Rh negative, few (including medical doctors) realize that "Rh" stands for rhesus monkey. In other words, if your blood is Rh positive, it means that your genetic structure is akin to that of the rhesus monkey.* Without the rhesus monkey factor, there is no logical reason to assume that the genetics of these people must have originated on the Earth. Reports have surfaced that governments have done covert research on Rh negative blood just to study these factors. The message in all of this is clear: the Gaelic race and/or whoever else has Rh negative blood may well have descended from ancient Martians.

There is also some hope for those of us who have Rh positive blood. We may be Martians too. According to the book *GENESET* by David Wood and Ian Campbell (published by Bellevue Books in England), studies were done on human

---

* None of this is meant to suggest that you yourself were derived from apes, but if you suddenly feel an incessant craving for bananas or the desire to swing from trees, be calm. It is just your genetic memory coming awake and it will soon pass.

beings subjected to complete sensory deprivation in a flotation tank. After a period of time by various individuals in the tank, the body clocks which control all the autonomous nervous systems all returned to a cycle of 24 hours and forty minutes. This is the length of a Martian day! If this is the case, then maybe our entire genetics originated from Mars when it occupied the cradle orbit.

All of this talk of Martian blood will certainly bring to mind for some the legends of the Merovingian dynasty that settled in the south of France and were known as the Cathars. According to the book *Holy Blood, Holy Grail*, these people were believed to have descended from the family of Jesus. Some theories even contend that Jesus himself lived and escaped to the south of France with Mary Magdalene. The Cathars were virtually wiped out by the inquisition, but they carried forth a legacy that is well known by the crown heads of Europe: blue-blood descends from the House of David (of which Jesus was recorded to be a part). Our question now becomes: was it Martian blood?

One thing is certain. The Cathars were not politically powerful enough to stand up to the Pope. They could not overtly claim lineage to Jesus whether true or not. They had to go underground and as a result developed "Grail Christianity" which taught the ancient mysteries in the form of Christianized legends. For the most part, this tact escaped the wrath of the Church. The Grail movement peaked with the legends of King Arthur and the Knights of the Round Table. These knights pursued the Holy Grail which they believed to contain the blood of Christ. Their kingdom was known as Camelot which itself means Martian City or City of Mars.*

There is one other aspect we should touch on when we consider blood. The derivation of the word comes from the Indo-European root *bhlo* which means to sprout or bloom. The idea being put forth is that of a crystalline growth matrix and

---

* Credit on this point goes to Jon Singer who researched that Camelot derives from Camulodunum which is a Celto-Latin word. Cumhul = Gaulish Celtic god whom the Romans called Mars. Dunum = city.

this brings us back to the concept of sacred geometry and the flower of life principle.

As one continues to study these various legends that have been offered about Mars, the blood of Christ and what not, their relative truth becomes less significant when we consider the actual communications and principles that are encoded in the words and language being used. Still, most people have had little time to consider these different legends, let alone the encodements of esoterica. The fact is, the history given here has previously been denied to the masses. That it was so denied has created a curious colloquialism in our culture. In the United States, it is common for people to describe someone who is impossible to relate to as "Martian". Sometimes they will say, "He/She is totally Martian". This is a subtle psychological and covert manipulation of consciousness that has been laced throughout the speech of our culture. If it comes from Mars, it couldn't possibly have any credibility. Ridicule is one of the first lines of disinformation. It means that someone doesn't want you to further investigate the subject at hand.

18

MARTIAN LEGACY

In many respects, modern UFOlogy began in the 1940s with the contacts of George Hunt Williamson and George Adamski. Williamson was a professor of archaeology who allegedly inspired the character Indiana Jones and left behind a legacy of information concerning Mars. As contacts and abductions weren't taken too seriously during his life, his experiences and discoveries were ignored.

Williamson taught archaeology at the University of Colorado but lost his professorship because he wrote about UFOs and expressed contrarian views. Much of his controversial information concerned the legend of a Martian colony sent to Earth.

According to this account, the race that initially settled Earth was called the Elder Race or Elohim (which means first born) and it was their intention to evolve on this planet. At that time, the existing race on Earth was barely erect and not very evolved.*

The Elohim were highly technical. Although they were not very spiritually evolved, they knew that was their next step and expected it would take them many many years to make serious progress in that direction. They called themselves

---

* It has been speculated by some that the Elohim took steps over a long period to ensure that the dinosaurs would vanish. This was a creational process designed to make the planet inhabitable for the various human races.

131

"human" because the word "HU" in their language stood for what they termed "the full array of color of God". They considered the entire electromagnetic spectrum to be the total frequency of God. "Hu" is a perfect homonym for the word "hue" and it stands to reason that this is the actual derivation of the word "human".

According to Williamson's account, the Elohim had colonized Mars before Earth and left behind a written history of their life on that planet. At one point, when Mars was in the cradle orbit, different life forms existed on the planet's surface. As the orbit changed, Mars developed an unsteady climate. Freezing and thawing were rapid and occurred frequently. Floods widened the canals that existed. All of this took its toll on the population, hence a decision was made to transmigrate off the planet. Those who had evolved spiritually were able to shift their modality of existence and stayed in the locale of Mars except that they were in another dimension, not unlike the Martians in Ray Bradbury's *Martian Chronicles*. Those who could not had to rely on exoteric means to stay alive. This meant using time travel machines or space craft and moving to Earth in a physical form. It would also include those who reincarnated from a Martian body to an Earth body.

All in all, Williamson had an incredible story to tell and it matches up nicely with what was discussed in the last chapter. Of considerably more interest were his claims that a vast array of information was written in "scrolls" that were actually geometric symbols "etched" in crystals. This format is quite ironic because it is very similar to the Eloi's (note the similarity of this word to Elohim) magic library of crystals that was referred to in H.G. Wells' *Time Machine*. Actually, Williamson's "etchings" weren't etchings at all. They were tiny geometric patterns formed by auditory tones. To the naked eye, they appeared as flaws in the crystal. A microscope would reveal something totally different.

George Hunt Williamson has been credited by some as one of the first layman allowed to penetrate past the ancient gates of wisdom and meet with the "keepers of the gate". He had learned of these crystals in the Andes through the original Monastary of the Seven Rays. As would be expected, quite an insurgence of interest was aroused when he emerged into the realm of the public and began to tell his incredible story. There was a ready audience wanting to know the actual nature of these mystery schools and what adeptship really meant. All of this intrigue included the initiatory processes that had been popular in Madame Blavatsky's days. It pointed to the Egyptians, the Atlanteans, the Sirians and other movements that were supposedly key to creating different branches of mystery schools.

During the same general period in which Williamson was receiving his contacts, there was a sudden resurgence on the other side of the planet with respect to Mars. The Third Reich had discovered another aspect of Martian history through their archaeological searches in Tibet. Various artifacts revealed a history of what was first established on Mars. Interestingly, they corresponded to Williamson's discoveries in the Andes. According to Williamson, these records date back 450,000 years with the oldest possibly being over one million years old. He was particularly struck by the fact that the natives in the Andes drew maps of Mars on their pottery that mimicked the geographical locations on the surface of the planet.

In both South America and the Far East, the most important information in these artifacts were crystal tablets which illustrated techniques designed to uplift the consciousness of mankind. These included geometrical representations in two dimensional form that were designed to be viewed three dimensionally and thereby invoke a fourth dimensional experience or transcendence. Each separate design was a process in itself that was in effect its own school of thought. When one process was completed, one would then in turn move on to the next.

Artifacts of this nature were routinely hidden in what were called "the secret places of the lion". This is the basis for seeing lions (both western and flamboyant oriental versions) guarding doorways to buildings. Of all these locations, the most sacred place and one that still cannot be accessed (physically or interdimensionally) at this particular point in time are the pyramids at Shensi. These are located in China, just outside of Tibet. At Shensi, there are ten major pyramids, three smaller ones and three types of sphinxes. The Third Reich's influence in this area was supplanted when Mao Tse Tung's army took over Tibet and ran their campaign of oppression and slaughtered monks on a wholesale basis. There were obviously multiple motivations involved when you consider the implication of the Shensi pyramids. The territory became off limits and still is to this day.

According to Williamson, these pyramids were the last seal to be broken on this planet. If they could be opened, a lost science would be rediscovered on how to tap into the Earth grid itself. This not only implied the advent of free energy but an entire shift in consciousness for humanity. When the Nazis learned of this through the Tibetans, the slaughter of the monks began.

That these tablets could have come from Mars could be considered hard to accept from what is considered to be "normal American thought" at this particular time. Keeping in mind the earlier correspondences between Mars and Cairo, it shouldn't be surprising that these same lessons were found to exist in Egypt.

19

LOST WISDOM

Earlier, it was mentioned that there is an actual inverted pyramid constructed underneath the Great Pyramid at Giza. If you descend into this region, there is an underground pathway to the Sphinx. This structure is approximately 39,000 years old, the same age as the Shensi pyramids. Known as the Hall of Records, this pathway contained wall inscriptions of sacred geometrical symbols that had been handed down during the time of Tahuti. These symbols were his law which was known as "The Law of One" and eventually became known as the mystery schools of the Eyes of Horus.

In Egyptian mythology, Horus was the son of Osiris and Isis and the brother of Set or Seth. Osiris was murdered by Set who cut his body into fourteen pieces and scattered them across the Earth. Isis was grief stricken but gathered all the pieces except for the penis. Her son, Horus, avenged his father by killing Set and finding his father's penis. Then, Osiris was resurrected and took his place as lord of the underworld and judged the dead for their next incarnation. Horus then assumed the throne of the outer world.

This myth contains interesting symbology just in the geometry alone. The thirteen pieces of Osiris's body represent the close packing of spheres whereby twelve spheres fit snugly and geometrically equidistant around the one. The fourteenth piece represents the fourteen faces that form around the packed

135

spheres when they are surrounded by a flat plane surface. Because his body was cut into thirteen pieces, Osiris assumed the role of lord of the underworld because there are thirteen spheres below the plane surfaces. Horus found the fourteenth piece of his father's body and accordingly assumed the throne of the outer world.

As was stated earlier, Tahuti had many roles in mythology. He also served as the physician of the eye of Horus. In various stories, Horus would lose his eye and Tahuti would repair it. He did this for other gods as well and could well be considered a doctor of perception. As the geometry of evolution would unfold, mistakes were made and Tahuti was the function that would correct them.

It was this concept of improving perception that led to the schools of the Eye of Horus. These schools were divided into the Right Eye of Horus and the Left Eye of Horus. In physiology, the right eye corresponds to the left side of the brain which is the intellectual, linear or analogical side. Accordingly, the Right Eye of Horus concerned itself with those aspects of human function. As the left eye corresponds to the right side of the brain which is intuitive or creative in aspect, the Left Eye of Horus concerned itself with that.

The purpose of the schools of the Eye of Horus were to eventually fuse the crystalline structure of one side of the brain with the other. When one actually achieved this, a white powder of gold was secreted out of the forehead during the initiatory rites. This was also known as the Illumination of the Eye of Horus or the opening of the third eye. What was happening was that a chemical process in the pituitary of the brain was cascading hormones through the area known as the third eye. All of the various initiatory rites were done in a manner so as to promote a harmonic relationship between the energy fields of the body and the Earth grid. The word "hormone" itself is suspiciously close to and in all likelihood derives from the word "harmonic" (dictionaries do not seem to recognize this). The initiatory rites addressed the seven seals of the body (the endocrine or ductless glands) which correspond to the seven chakras. These rites climaxed with the seventh or last seal being broken. All of this equated to what was called "the opening of the great book" and resulted in a right angle shift of consciousness or transcendental experience of leaving the body.

The above account is very intriguing and tells us that at one time in history there was a precise procedure that was designed to enable one to rise out of the body and reach out towards the full potential of the human spirit. All of this gives rise to different questions. First, what were the techniques? And, if they were so good, why did the people who are presumed to have used them fail to make them known to the rest of the world?

The answer to these questions lies in the very rhythms of the orbital mechanics of our Earth and solar system, particularly as they relate to the center of our galaxy. First, we will relate how these orbital mechanics expressed themselves in terms of social consciousness.

There was a time in history when we were very advanced and various wisdom was readily accessible to all who desired it. But, it was eventually decided to keep the wisdom locked up in temples under the guise of priesthoods. The keepers of such wisdom became very obscure. Lao Tzu became one of the most notable examples. According to legend, he was a sage who decided to leave society. As he passed out of civilization, the gate keeper stopped him and insisted he write down his insights on paper. This became known as the *Tao Te Ching* or the *Book of the Tao*. Lao Tzu then retired into the forest and was never seen again. In light of the other data in this book, it is clear that Lao Tzu pierced the veil of this dimension and actually left it. The famous gate keeper of Chinese legend is an obvious analogy to the gate keepers of this dimension. If one studies Taoism as laid down by Lao Tzu and the legends concerning him, one discovers that his main attribute was neither wisdom, virtue nor perception. It was obscurity! This had everything to do with the consciousness of the times which, believe it or not, is actually based upon hyperdimensional physics. An explanation follows.

As the moon and Earth revolve around the sun, so does our entire solar system orbit the galactic center of our universe which is sometimes known as the Black Sun or our zero point reference mark. Every 26,000 years (this number is an approximation) there is an occurrence on Earth known as the Precession of the Equinoxes. This event refers to the fact that every sidereal year the exact point of the equinox, as gauged against the night sky, moves a little bit westward on the horizon. For example, if you were looking at the horizon on the spring equinox and saw the constellation Aries, it would appear in location X. The next year on the spring equinox, it would appear just a little bit westward but not enough to be noticed by the naked eye. The reason it moves is due to a slight gravitational pull on the Earth from the sun and moon. This tilts the Earth's axis and causes it to appear to wobble a little, but over a period of 26,000 years the gradual western movement of the equinox will come full circle and it will end up in exactly the same place it started. This movement of 26,000 years is called a yuga.

As the axis of our Earth tilts during a yuga, it will be spinning towards the black sun for one half of the yuga and away from the black sun for the other half. The black sun is the source of light in our local universe. The spin away from the black sun is termed a negative spin because we are tilted away from the light source. The duration of the half yuga when we are tilted toward the black sun is termed a positive spin. Each half yuga is 13,000 years.

What all of this means in terms of universal correspondence is that the very spin of the electrons changes from one half-yuga to the next. In other words, the electrons inside the atoms that compose our physical world spin towards the light during the Earth's tilt toward the light. During the spin away from the light, the same atoms spin towards the darkness. In terms of evolution, light would be evolutionary and darkness, or a negative spin, would be involutionary.

At this writing, we are just moving into the Age of Aquarius and are beginning our spin towards the light center. The veils of darkness are beginning to clear, hence information like this is now becoming available in many quarters. In times past, priesthoods sequestered sacred knowledge as we moved away from the center of light. Unfortunately, the priesthoods went overboard and a major involution of consciousness occurred. Of course, you don't totally lose everything and it is still possible for us now to regain all of our lost heritage.

The repercussions of this major shift have not fully impacted us as of yet. Several Earth changes have already been witnessed as of the publication date of this book and some people even anticipate a major pole shift. There are many theories of what is going to take place but it is not necessary to indulge in speculation. There are plenty of others doing that.

There is another very important aspect to mention as regards what happens when a yuga shifts from a dark spin to a light spin. This has been charted by many different scientific studies (including extensive work at Stanford University) and concerns the magnetic properties of the dipoles of the brain. Because the brain functions like computer bits based on bioelectromagnetic fields, the entire memory of a being can be stripped when the magnetic field of the earth loses its intensity or is otherwise affected. This is exactly what happens during a yuga shift which we are on the verge of reaching right now.

The mystery schools have played an important part in history with regard to the above as their goal was always to maintain a continuity of thought. This includes the process of self remembrance from life to life. Of course, this type of situation has resulted in only a select few of the human race remembering anything with secret societies like the Illuminati contracting with other forces to take advantage of implanting and thereby sequestering power for their own ends.

If the magnetic grid goes down to zero, we are all endangered of losing our memory. For some, it could be totally wiped out. But, it is possible to combat such a catastrophe by utilizing the very electromagnetic fiber "of which you are made". By learning how to communicate with your own electromagnetic fields, you can alter and rotate your fields in such a manner so as to retain your own magnetism. All of these fields correspond to geometric shapes but it is an extensive subject and beyond the scope of this present work.

The Sphinx was designed to play a very important role in helping us to retain our memory. As the various eras of evolution end, they are in a sense "written up" and referred to the data base which we have been referring to as the morpho-genetic grid. This information is then by matter of long standing universal custom deposited in the Hall of Records adjacent to the Sphinx. Both the past and the future are stored here and can be consulted for the next cycle of evolution. In this manner, the Hall of Records established an educational process through which we could know what our evolution was going to be. At the end of a yuga, the records are designed to be tapped so as to tell us our direction and to remind us of the ancient wisdom of the past.

It becomes obvious sooner or later that immortality (in terms of memory if not necessarily the body) is a big issue concerning the Hall of Records. If one can tap the records, they achieve immortality which is the same thing as continuity of memory. It also becomes possible to transcend into the next level of consciousness. As mentioned above, this becomes an area of contention with the mystery schools and a power elite of which certain international bankers are just a front guard.

A quick view of history can clue one in on what is being said here. Civilizations have always been known to have sudden rises in their society and then a long period of decline with very little evolution occurring. This is all in tune with the cycles of moving away from the galactic center and then moving towards the galactic center. When the Sphinx was created, if you turn the clock backwards, you'll be able to understand how the rise of civilization reached a great peak and then 13,000 years later began to decline. This was a repetitive pattern with the last period being the final destruction of Atlantis 13,000 years ago. Of course, the memory of the culture was destroyed too.

In this manner, the mystery schools retained their key secret: the idea that you could contain your own magnetic field in what is called the egg or merkabah* by rotating geometric symbols (that in fact are senior to your electromagnetic field) in a visualization process so as to set up one's own merkabah.

The grand design and the purpose of pursuing these mysteries is to reach our highest state of evolution. When we finally reach such a peak, it is said that the records will be put into place and we will begin our transmigration off this planet.

If all the information given in this book is generally correct, it suggests we will be bombarded with various information that has remained buried for millennia. If this is true, we have much reason to hope that the Age of Aquarius will be one of true enlightenment and understanding. Although we might find that incredible information is in ample supply, we would all be foolish to think that everything is going to come to us automatically with no effort on our part. But there does seem to be plenty of optimism for those of us who want to learn from our ancient past and program our future accordingly.

As this book is being written, we are approaching the "end times". New Agers tend to cite the Mayan calendar ending in 2012 and Christians remind us of the Apocalypse and Armageddon. Regardless of what you hear or believe, I'm sure you will agree that plenty of trash is being circulated about the phenomena that might occur at the "end times". Many people try to foster the fear that the world will suffer severe Earth changes and that most of the United States will fall into the ocean. Then, you see the same people selling real estate in Montana to gullible listeners. You have to wonder.

By examining certain aspects of the past, we might gain some perspective for the future. Accordingly, we will now begin a short view of history that will lead us back to Montauk and some major planetary influences.

---

* Merkabah is derived from Mer = life force (it also means to think or remember), ka = soul, and bah = vehicle to carry (the soul). Put together, it is the vehicle to carry the soul and is also recognized as an interdimensional vehicle, i.e. one uses the merkabah when one wants to travel from one dimension to another.

20

PHREES AND CATHOLIES

In accordance with the yuga theory we have just discussed, Earth civilization reached its last peak during Atlantean
times about 13,000 years ago. During that time period society
was closely related to Solomon's Republic where all citizens
were of equal importance whether laborer or scholar. Everyone
was schooled in wisdom and graduated with entire degrees of
knowledge which included all aspects of awareness. This was
a much higher state than what we know today. As the energy
fields began a negative spin, society began to decline. People
realized they did have some empowerment but not necessarily
the wisdom or the energy gained from the light entropy that was
moving away from the galactic center. As a result, a huge
polarity in consciousness was created. The new social consciousness was moving toward the dark. The Light Warriors
found themselves to be a dying breed. The evolution of the two
polarities eventually resulted in two main factions: the Phrees
and the Catholies.

"Phree" is a French word for light. This means that the
Phrees identified themselves as light builders or Freemasons.
"Catholie" comes from the root "catholic" which means universal or completely whole. Both of these factions had originally
evolved from the ancient wisdom schools that had existed in
Lemuria. At that time there was a "citizenship of consciousness" on the planet. Everyone was more or less attuned and

operating on the same frequency. This was disrupted during the cataclysmic shifting of land masses that occurred and both groups manifested as a result of the break up. The dark yuga was gaining ground with two factions instead of one universal brotherhood.

While the Phrees called themselves light builders, the Catholies assumed they were as well. They were more concerned with control and reattaining a universal consciousness on the planet. The Phrees tended to view the universalists as a controlling dark force and sought out independence and secret truth. They would carry the flame for a future time. Both schools were renegade groups cut from the same cloth. The important factor was that they were polarized and in competition. This was a step down from the previous consciousness that had prevailed during the light yuga. The result of all this was the creation of religious systems that in turn created illusionary processes that gave one a reason to abandon one's free will and turn it over to a belief system. In such an atmosphere the Phrees emerged into Egypt and Catholies into Italy, giving rise to Julius Caesar and the Roman Empire.

The Phrees regarded their knowledge of the light so valuable, they kept it secret in an effort to preserve it. This unwittingly resulted in them preserving it so well that no one knew it or practiced it. The Catholies were universalists and wanted to unite everything under one banner. Being more aggressive, they won the war with Egypt.

Of course, the Phrees and Catholies didn't begin in Egypt and Italy. As said earlier, their history goes way back. But, the emergence of these groups around the year zero is very important for this time period was a turning point in our consciousness of time.

21

A SHORT HISTORY OF THE WORLD

The short history of the world that follows in this chapter begins about the year zero. It is not meant to be a complete or even authoritative view on the world. It is based upon my own general readings and personal conclusions but it is written here for two reasons. First and most important, it will demonstrate how the Phrees and Catholies can interface with our reality so as to vie for control. Second, it serves as a time reference point between the ancient history previously discussed and our investigation of Montauk.

According to one source, the time period just after the year zero was filled with so much shock and astonishment that the people who witnessed the events never fully recovered. Whatever happened during the life of Jesus was only written down (at least for general public consumption) many years later. To say that it was all the result of a space ship here and an alien there is an over simplification and not particularly true. It was obviously a time period where interdimensionality was at the forefront of the consciousness of man. Regardless of what actually happened during the Christ saga, it is a certainty that afterwards general consciousness drifted away from the kingdom of heaven (or higher dimensions if you prefer) and proceeded towards the dark ages.

At the height of the Roman Empire, the Romans were

famous for "Romanizing" their enemies. In other words, they would teach conquered people their law, finance systems and customs and so strengthen their hold on their empire. After Christ, the Catholies maintained Roman power by absorbing Christianity into their empire. The early Christian teachings were virtually identical to those taught in Egypt and were a threat to the Roman Empire. Both movements were consolidated when Constantine issued the Edict of Milan and allowed Roman citizens to freely worship Christ. The Phrees and Catholies were actually united to some degree and a monopoly was achieved that would remain in place for a long time. Despite the political success of Constantine, he aroused the ire of the intelligentsia when he established the Council of Nicea which forbade the doctrine of reincarnation and short circuited everyone's attention to the Holy Trinity. The resultant effect was a prohibition on memory with seekers of truth and enlightenment going underground.

The most significant of the underground groups that carried the torch of the Phrees during this period were the Gnostics. They continued to practice their own beliefs despite harassment from the Church. They were among the first heretics. Rising from the tradition of the Gnostics was Charlemagne, the first Emperor of the Holy Roman Empire. He came to power around 700 A.D. and sought to break the monopoly that the Catholies held under the guise of the Roman Catholic Church. He passionately participated in and oversaw the Grail Christianity movement which sought to teach the ancient mysteries and was in direct opposition to the Church. After much intrigue and political skirmishes, Charlemagne was forced to kneel and kiss the Pope's ring. It was a most dramatic and historic gesture. The Holy Roman Empire survived in namesake only. The Pope held the stronger political cards. Although Charlemagne could not buck the power of the Pope completely, he continued to carry the Spear of Longinus (the spear believed to have pierced the side of Christ) as a magical talisman and fostered the ancient mysteries in secret. One day, at the advanced age of seventy-two, Charlemagne dropped the spear from his horse. It was

146

viewed as an omen by his soldiers and he died within two weeks. Whoever possessed that spear afterwards was thought to control the destiny of mankind for good or for evil. Although Charlemagne died and did not achieve complete freedom from the Church, his own efforts would eventually climax with the Age of Chivalry and King Arthur.

Even before Charlemagne was born, there were elements trying hard to pierce the armor of the Catholie/Phree consolidation. In 570 A.D., the Prophet of Islam was born. He would rise to unite the warring Arab tribes under the will of Allah. These efforts could be interpreted as an attempt by a higher power to thwart the establishment of the Catholies who possessed the Holy Land. The Prophet, a Phree, conquered Jerusalem and delivered it from Christian hands. Just when the Phrees thought they had won a major battle, the Prophet gave way to old age and his own heirs were deposed. The Catholies took over the Islamic movement at that point and controlled the Holy Land once more only this time under a different banner.

It is interesting and important to note that the Prophet received his transmissions for the Q'ran from Gabriel, the archangel of good news. As a messenger of news, Gabriel cabalistically corresponds with Tahuti, the author of the Hall of Records, which in turn tells us who was directing this movement. The bloodline of the Prophet's family was never obliterated. Always considered a renegade sect from mainstream Islam, his latter day descendants live in the haven for all political refugees: France, the land of the Phrees.

At this point, the Catholies controlled the Holy Land but the situation was almost comical. The Phrees took advantage of the situation and sold the entire European continent on the idea of the Crusades. Huge armies arose in the name of Christ in order to wrest the Holy Land from the Moslems. Even children took arms senselessly in what could have been an early forerunner of the Montauk boys project. The legend of the Pied Piper arose from the rampant child abuse of this period.

The Phrees were playing both sides from the very beginning and actually emerged as major players in the form of the

Knights Templars. Their beliefs are too intricate to go into here but they fostered a legend that Jesus did not die on the cross, but instead escaped with his family to southern France, taking with him the ancient wisdom of Egypt and Moses. Their ancestors became known as the Cathars (an ironic phonetic spelling) and were heavily persecuted and virtually exterminated during the Inquisition.

The Knights Templars first became popular by offering tours to the Holy Land. As they were tough soldiers and had intimate connections to the Moslems who governed Jerusalem, people felt safe to visit the various Christian shrines under their guardianship. The tours to these sacred places were quite costly with both the Templars and cooperating Muslims profiting handsomely. The Templars became extremely wealthy as a result and started the basic structure of what would eventually become international banking. When the Crusades actually turned the Holy Land back over to the Christians for a short while, the Templars became the physical guardians of the Holy Sepulcher from which they derived their name (the Knights of the Temple).

After amassing tremendous wealth and power, the Templars became too conspicuous for their own good. King Phillip of France sought refuge from a mob in their Parisian temple. Amazed at their wealth, the king later applied for membership with the Templars but was denied. Consequently, he conspired with the Pope to outlaw the Templars, who had become a formidable political threat to the Church itself, and made them the major target of the Inquisition. Jacque De Molay, the titular head of the Templars, was arrested but many escaped to Scotland and took most of the order's wealth with them.

De Molay was literally roasted over a fire. As he cooked, he placed a curse on the King in public and said he would die within a prescribed time period. Only a matter of months later, King Phillip died and an assault was begun on the French monarchy that hundreds of years later led to the storming of the bastille and the guillotining of Marie Antoinette. Very close ties between Scotland and France have existed ever since the burning of Jacque De Molay.

Napoleon arose from the ashes of the French Revolution and his first action was to insult the Pope. He then conquered Egypt and sought out its sacred wisdom. This is an untold portion of history. Napoleon also made efforts to acquire the Spear of Longinus that Charlemagne had possessed, but almost the entire Phree society of Europe successfully conspired to keep it out of his hands. Although he appeared like a Phree when he insulted the Pope, he also sought total unification of the world which was a Catholie precept. Napoleon was complex and was used by both sides. He was eventually poisoned on the island of St. Helena (a volcanic island and major grid point connected to Atlantis). Arsenic was discovered in a hair analysis and his death was probably caused to keep him quiet.

It was during the time of Napoleon that a major Jewish faction rose to prominence on the world scene. This was the Rothschild family. Both Christianity and Islam had evolved out of the Jewish religion, but the Jews had lost power in their homeland and had become a wandering tribe again. The monarchies of Europe had never been particularly sympathetic towards the Jews and the slightest transgression or misunderstanding could quickly lead to enmity. It was in such an atmosphere that the Rothschild's began to play one monarchy against the other and build a Jewish power base in the form of international banking. This was pure racial survival on their part. They were also able to ostensibly replace the banking functions that the Knights Templars had carried out in society before being forced to go underground.

Additionally, the Rothschild family orchestrated the entire Battle of Waterloo (and probably influenced Napoleon's escape from Elba) so as to make an absolute killing on the London Stock Exchange. Rothschild, being Jewish, was sympathetic with the Phrees for it was the Catholie establishment he way trying to bowl over. What is ironic here is that the monarchies were Catholie oriented as they paid homage to the Pope and bowed to his authority. But, in secret, most of the monarchies secretly subscribed to the Cathars and believe their "blue blood" descended from the lineage of Christ himself.

The subtleties and interplay between the Phrees and Catholics is so complex as to be endless. The lesson is that the social consciousness of the times were such that polarity was the watchword. Who was right is not important. People were divided against each other and the war god Mars seemed to be predominant in everyone's activity. In Viking mythology, you went to heaven if you died in battle but you descended into hell if you died outside the battlefield.

The Knights Templars regrouped in Scotland and there was tremendous fighting between this faction and the Crown of England who were just beginning to thrive as the Catholic British Empire. At this time, the Templars were actually augmenting an ancient legacy that was known as the Jacobite Rebellion.

The Jacobites had originated in Asia Minor and were Gnostic in their orientation. They had migrated to the British Isles as part of the Celtic movement described elsewhere in this book. They not only claimed Pharaonic heritage from Egypt but opposed what they considered to be the sterile teachings of the Church. Britain was predominantly a pagan land and the old religion of the Druids still touched the hearts of the people. The Roman legions had first conquered the Britons and established Catholic law. Henry VIII established the Church of England in an apparent break from the Catholic empire. This gave hope to the early protestant movement, but the Church of England ultimately remained very much a Catholic institution. One of its main purposes seemed to be to keep the ancient Celtic beliefs (and Phrees) in check.

King James II (also known as King James VII of Scotland) was considered by the Jacobites to be the last legal and rightful King of Great Britain. Part of this legacy has to do with the Stone of Scone over which all rightful kings were coronated. It possessed magical properties and was contained in an abbey in E. Perthshire, Scotland. Edward I absconded with the stone and had it placed under the coronation chair at Westminster Abbey.

In this manner, the Kings of England "stole" the Scottish kingdom.

All of this came to a head after James II. His family were known as the Stuarts and their rightful heir to the throne was Bonnie Prince Charlie who had hidden in France after the family had been stripped of power in England. Bonnie Prince Charlie made a noble comeback and at one point actually raised an army of 5,000 that began a march into London. Although he was overmatched by a nearby army of 10,000 and 30,000 additional troops were awaiting him outside London, history records that the English Crown had ignited panic throughout all London. The people despised the English monarchy and the king knew this. So did Bonnie Prince Charlie who fearlessly continued his march on London. He had good reason to believe that the common people would join his noble and pagan cause and overthrow the king's army. He was probably right as he was the only symbol the native Britons could rally around. Unfortunately for him, his advisors were either cowards and/or spies and more or less overruled him from continuing on into the heart of the city. He retreated and had to hide evermore. The English pursued him throughout Scotland and his life was saved by a Duncan Cameron when he had fallen off a cliff. The Camerons and the Mar family (who resided in Mar, a district in Aberdeenshire, Scotland. Mar was also a title given to saints and clergy in the Jacobite Church.) were both extremely influential in helping Bonnie Prince Charlie survive and keeping the light of the Phrees shining.

One of the more amusing incidents in the flight of Bonnie Prince Charlie is when he hides in the Isle of Skye near Dun Cann, a volcanic conical hill that is truncated at the top. The etymology of Dun Cann is interesting because in one sense Dun means horse and cann means power. This corresponds with the golden horse on the cover of *The Montauk Project* which was a vehicle for time travel. In another sense, "dun" means a hill fortress just like the word "Montauk" has been defined by some. In this sense "Dun Cann" would mean powerful fortress.

Perhaps the most intriguing etymology of the word "Dun

Cann" is the basic English where "dun" means twilight and "Cann" either 1) power or ability to translate into the physical world, 2) a tube or reed or 3) colorful or chromatic display. "Dun" is the world of twilight between dark and light. "Cann" is the tube or channel between worlds and could also serve as the full electromagnetic spectrum which represents the full array of creation.

Not long after the Templars moved to the British Isles and just before the flight of Bonnie Prince Charlie, the Crowleys, Parsons and Wilsons migrated to America and settled in the Massachusetts Bay Colony. Some were reported to have been on the Mayflower. The Cameron clan couldn't have been too far behind. Other families were involved, of course, and Freemasonry began to take root in America.

In a book on the Parsons family lineage, the Parsons claim to have been close personal friends of George Washington, a Master Mason, and decided to help the country's cause in an inauspicious manner. Although very influential, the Parsons found it best not to carry a high profile. One of the Wilson clan, a James Wilson, is reported to have authored most of the U.S. Constitution. Of course, he would have known Thomas Jefferson personally, the self appointed curator of the Montauk Indians' native tongue.

Thomas Jefferson and Ben Franklin served as ambassadors to France and had very strong ties to the Phrees of that country. In one biography of Jefferson, he had a mistress who had previously been involved romantically with a mysterious Dr. Parsons (nothing else was said about him). As President, Jefferson made the Louisiana Purchase from France on very favorable terms. Less than one hundred years later, the Statue of Liberty was an open thanks of gratitude from the Phrees of France to the Phrees of America. A new colony of freedom, in the tradition of the Phrees, had been established.

Although freedom was won in America, the Catholies sought to break this up when the British Crown financed the Civil War in an effort to break up the United States. When that failed, the Catholies began to use financial means to establish their position of total unity. Rockefeller began to rise in the oil industry and this industry is still used in the world as a major political tool to this day.

World War I was inspired in no small part as a result of the animosity between the British Catholies and the native Europeans sentiment toward the old Holy Roman Empire. At this time, the British certainly had an economic strangle hold on Europe if not the entire world. The Rothschild family who had earlier been sympathetic towards the Phrees when it suited their cause, embraced the British Empire in what the Germans considered the rape of Europe. A war had been successfully orchestrated that left the Germans in economic slavery to the British Empire and their connected banking interests.

Everything climaxed when Hitler successfully acquired the Spear of Longinus, the same one that Charlemagne had possessed. Only after obtaining that talisman did he seriously embark upon his military conquests. He was the ultimate Catholie, seeking to unite the entire world under one of the most sacred symbols of mankind: the swastika. Of course, today the swastika is not considered sacred at all but is thought to be a symbol of anti-Semitism. That is not the way it was intended by the ancients. It derives from the Sanskrit word *svasti* and means well-being or benediction. The Nazis are thought to have reversed the direction of the swastika, but it actually appears both ways in ancient artifacts. What is most interesting about the swastika is that its legs make ninety degree angles with respect to its central cross of space and time. This is meant to represent a shift in consciousness. Despite the fact that Hitler has been labeled as a complete lunatic, he knew the esoteric meanings of these symbols and was said to know scripture better than any of the priests or religious men who frequented the beer gardens of Munich.

Hitler could not rely totally on archetypal symbols that reached deep into the collective consciousness of mankind and the morphogenetic grid. He also needed a real life enemy to unite the people against. In the grand scheme of the world, the Jewish bankers fit the bill he needed. They were a perfect sociological target for Hitler's mentality and that of the Aryan race at that time period. Hitler, who was himself part Jewish, played upon the sympathies against the Jews which have always run somewhat rampant among the European Aryans. In the early years of Hitler's power, the Jews were encouraged to leave Germany. They were not forced. One Jewish representative even obtained a list of Jewish names and address from the Gestapo in order to help them emigrate. Later on, all the Jews were persecuted mercilessly and the holocaust ensued but not until their power base in Germany was nullified.

With Hitler, the Yuga had reached its darkest hour. Within hours of his officially reported death, the Spear of Longinus was discovered in a vault by American troops and came into the possession of the Allied Command. Eventually, it was returned (some say it was a replica) to the Hapsburg museum in Vienna. The balance of power had shifted.

After winning World War II, the Allies inherited the Nazi war machine and intelligence service. They also acquired their genetic research, aerospace technology and an entire collection of esoteric relics and information. This transition of power was orchestrated by the Office of Strategic Services which eventually became the Central Intelligence Agency, the forward vanguard of this new age.

22

THE NAZI'S DARKEST HOUR

When the CIA inherited the Nazi archives and personnel, they became the caretakers of a fascinating but dubious legacy. A person highly placed in the Church of England once told me that when the Allies discovered the fourth dimensional nature of the Nazi's relics, they were shocked and dismayed. A decision was made to continue covert research into the paranormal phenomena but to avoid the subject completely during the war trials.

Although the Nazi's were an abomination to good taste and human decency, it will surprise many people to learn that the group which put the Nazi party together was based upon religious and spiritual constructs. This story, and the eventual disintegration of the Nazi empire, begins with one of the most influential and overlooked characters in the history of the Third Reich: Karl Haushofer.*

Not too much is written about Karl Haushofer although his name appears in many indexes in books about the Nazis. His biography is a very interesting omission in world history. We do know that he was an occultist and had a masterful grasp

---

* The name Haushofer in German is the equivalent of Householder in English which has ironic significance if you consider the etymology of the word Pharaoh that was previously discussed. Pharaoh = House = hiding place or temple = magic hiding place or magic temple.

of different languages that included German, Russian, English, French, Sanskrit and Japanese. He may have spoken Chinese and Tibetan as well. Haushofer served as a military attaché in Tokyo around the turn of the century where his linguistic ability enabled him to forge the connections that would eventually form the basis for the Axis alliance. He also spent considerable time in Tibet where he became a member of the Bon priesthood. Also known as the Yellow Caps* of Tibet, the Bons represented a shamanistic religion that preceded Tibetan Buddhism and was considered to be the father of all Tibetan religions. Tibet, as the highest upwelling of energy on planet Earth, is considered to be a major access point with respect to influencing the morphogenetic grid.**

Haushofer also had a distinguished military career. As a general in World War I, his prophetic abilities were legendary and served him well in battle. While commanding troops on the front, he was never hurt and was able to deploy his troops with remarkable precision amidst much chaos. He was highly decorated and admired. Rudolph Hess, later to become Deputy Fuhrer of the Nazi Party, served under General Haushofer and was very impressed by his superior.

After World War I, Haushofer began to institute directives he had received (spiritually or otherwise) from his contacts in Tibet. He gathered other occultists and influential people and formed two societies: the Thule Society and the Vril Society.

The Thule Society derived their name from the mythological land of Hyperborea which existed either within the North Pole or nearby, depending upon which version you read. Thule

---

* The Bons are specifically identified in most Nazi occult literature as Yellow Caps, however there are many books on the Bons which identify them as Red Caps. This confusion of identity simply shows their pervasive influence.

** According to *The Occult Conspiracy* by Michael Howard, Destiny Books, Haushofer met the famous occultist and intelligence agent G.I. Gurdjieff who instructed the Dalai Lama. Gurdjieff, who was known as Dorjieff to some (see Dusty Sklar's *The Nazis and the Occult*, Dorset Press) during this period, also was reported to have had contact with Joseph Stalin who had once been a boarder in the house of the Gurdjieff family.

was the capital city and the home of the Aryan race. In Greek mythology, the god Apollo was a Hyperborean who slew the Python, a giant serpent, and established the Oracle of Delphi in Greece. Pythia was his high priestess. Pythagoras, a major mystery school figure himself, was believed to have been taught by the Hyperborean Apollo or to have been an incarnation of him. Pythagoras taught his students how to evolve through the principles of sacred geometry.

The Thule Society was drawing on a very rich legacy. How much they knew is anyone's guess, but the Thule Society cannot simply be dismissed as just a bunch of Aryan fanatics as they are so often portrayed in books. There is, however, no question that they manipulated Aryan fanatics and appealed to the Aryan myth in order to reach their desired goals.

The Thule Society of that time had two distinct branches. One was the esoteric branch which was headed by Rudolph Steiner, a famous occultist and scientist. Steiner was an artistic and wonderful man who could have pioneered a renaissance if given the opportunity. The other branch of the Thule Society was the exoteric branch which consisted primarily of industrialists, bankers and enforcers like the Brown Shirts of the early Nazi days. Hitler was eventually chosen to head up the exoteric branch of the Thule Society and soon did away with Steiner's influence, literally chasing him out of the country.

At the same time that the Thule Society was being formed, Haushofer established the Vril Society which was concerned with establishing the ancient Atlantean culture and correcting the mistakes that occurred during that era. The word "vril" itself means psychic energy. Two particular psychics were employed by Haushofer who did readings and eventually made contact with alien forces who shared extensive UFO technology with them. Extensive plans and blueprints were made up and activated as early as the 1920s. It is said that the saucers constructed were very poor fighting machines as they were not flexible enough with their drives to hover over specific targets. The Vril Society was also secretive and were not necessarily pushing the war effort. Many of their secrets were kept from Hitler and other top Nazis.

Once the Thule and Vril Societies were set up and operating, Karl Haushofer continued to operate behind the scenes but also became a college professor at the University of Munich. Having received his doctorate near the beginning of World War I, Dr. Haushofer coined a brand new subject called Geopolitics. Rudolph Hess sought out his old general who he admired so much and became an avid pupil at the university. Hess was said to be completely enamored with his professor's intellectual leadership and occult knowledge. It was during this period in Munich that Hess discovered Adolf Hitler.

After the war, Hitler worked for army intelligence and infiltrated communist groups in Munich which were an actual threat to Germany's political power structure. After the army moved in on the communists, Hitler pointed to the key leaders in person whereupon they were taken away and shot. Hitler's prestige increased with this act and his presence in the beer halls became more prominent. He began to speak passionately about the plight of post war Germany. His grasp of political and esoteric matters was remarkable and he was known to out debate anyone who came his way including deeply religious men.

One day, Rudolph Hess heard Hitler speaking and was both impressed and puzzled. He thought Hitler was either a messiah or a madman but wasn't sure which. Hess saw great qualities of leadership in Hitler and brought him to the attention of Haushofer. All three men became friends.

In 1923, Hitler staged a big event which would be known ever after as the Munich Beer Hall Putsh. Hitler and a group of armed and loyal men attempted to physically overthrow the Bavarian government. They didn't get very far. As they marched forward in the street, the Bavarian army fired. Hitler was reportedly the first to run but many of his associates were shot. Hitler was arrested but Hess escaped into Austria. Hitler was tried and convicted but gave a remarkable oration at his sentencing. Haushofer was so impressed that he decided he had found a use for him as a German messiah. Hitler was sentenced to nine months in prison and Hess showed his loyalty to Hitler by returning to Germany and sharing a cell with him. Haushofer visited them both during this period and probably contributed at least one full chapter of Hitler's *Mein Kamph*. When Hitler was released from prison, Haushofer taught him to dress and paved his way to influence.

While Hitler was being primed for his mission, another remarkable event is said to have occurred in Germany in 1923. According to Maia Shamayyim of the Star of Isis Mystery School*, there was a massive time travel experiment which involved the Nazis. Maia channels Tahuti who she calls Thoth and was told that the time rift known to have existed at Montauk did not begin with the Philadelphia Experiment in 1943 but in 1923 when key members of the Thule Society collaborated with Aleister Crowley's Lodge, the Astrum Argentinum (Order of the Silver Star of Illuminati) and a hybrid project was created that was called the Phisummum. This project and the entire purpose of the secret order who controlled it was time travel. This secret order was known as the Order of the Black Sun.

As I am highly suspicious of channeled information, I later called Maia and asked her where she had heard about the Order of the Black Sun. I'd never heard of it before and at that time had not realized the the Black Sun stood for the center of the galaxy. Maia said she had no personal experience on whether the order existed nor had she read about it. It had just come up in a channeling session.

More information would be revealed about a year later when I would receive a fax from a man in Germany who said he had contacts with the Thule and Vril Societies and that they were still in existence today. He had a lot to tell me, but in his opinion the information was too sensitive to be put over the fax lines. It would have to wait for an in person visit. Almost six months later, I would meet with this man in a hotel room in

---

* Those who are interested in receiving more information about the Star of Isis Mystery School should enclose $5 and write to Maia Shamayyim, c/o General Delivery, Crestone, Colorado, 81131.

New Jersey and he would tell me an earful. He explained that most American literature on the Thule and Vril societies is inaccurate and supplied me with the information you have just read about them. In most literature, Haushofer is generally mentioned as a member of these societies, not the founder. The connection to Tibet is seldom made but sometimes alluded to at best. As he explained different secret societies in Germany, I interrupted him and asked if he had ever heard of the Order of the Black Sun. Yes, he said. That was what he was going to talk about next! The purpose here is not to go into the details of that but to confirm Maia's insight. We will now continue with her information.

In project Phisummum, the Order of the Black Sun wanted to retrieve the Holy Grail from a past century and put it into the hands of the groomer of the Antichrist. This was at best an attempt to balance the two forces and create a transdimensional consciousness. As part of this magical process, Aleister Crowley and other magicians participated. Some of them were high ranking Nazis. Sex magic was employed and the Spear of Longinus was supposedly used as a magical power source. The Order of the Black Sun stayed out of the antics but set it up so as to control the results.

A small but distorted window in time was created and they all began to feel the overwhelming power of such an operation. In that same year the master of the project, Dietrich Eckhart, died and his successors (possessing less understanding than he had) created a rift in time which extended to Philadelphia in 1943, Montauk in 1634, Bannock Hill in the time of Merlin and several other points in time.

The only other information we learn from Maia is that after the "time explosion" in 1923, a Dr. Karl Obermeyer stole a core chamber that housed certain crystals which were crucial to the project. The crystals had been created in a long and arduous process of separating elements, not unlike nuclear fission, only the atoms involved were manipulated into a black hole inversion.

All of this information corroborates what Preston Nichols

has heard through the grapevine for years: World War II was a war of time. The movie *Philadelphia Experiment II* also gives a scenario where the Nazis conquered time travel. Extensive information will have to come in as well as more research before the Nazi time travel possibilities can be coherently reviewed and commented upon. It is sufficiently important to point out here that there were deep mystical orders involved that were not fooling around and meant serious business.

These secret societies saw Hitler as a Moonchild or messiah that could be used to unite the world and rebuild the Tower of Babylon in order to unite consciousness with the most high. It was for this reason that the Swastika, which represented the well being of the most primal forces in man, was chosen.

According to legends in the UFO community, the Pleiadians had close ties to the Thule Society and had befriended Hitler. They supplied him with UFO technology which we eventually saw in the form of Foo Fighters witnessed across the European theater of World War II. My German contact told me that there are no references to the Pleiadians that he has ever seen in German literature. It appears to be an Americanism. He did say that the name of the aliens who contacted the Vril society were Aldeberans. An inspection of a star map reveals that these two systems are both near the constellation Taurus in the night sky.

As Hitler rose to power, Karl Haushofer was granted any resources that he needed. He established the doctrines of Nazi academe and has been credited with designing the plan for the Germano-Japanese domination of the world. The name "Axis", which referred to the German-Japanese-Italian alliance, was based upon the shift of the Earth's axis (as was discussed earlier with regard to the Precession of the Equinoxes and the yuga) and its consequent correspondences to other heavenly bodies such as the black sun in the center of the galaxy. As stated earlier in this book, the center of the galaxy is referenced to zero time. Don't think that Haushofer didn't know this. Here was a brilliant man who had ostensibly orchestrated the discovery of sacred tablets in Tibet and wanted to bring the world back to its divine roots. He acted both like a Phree and a Catholie and is perhaps the best example of that dichotomy blending together. There was however a major reason for his failure: Adolf Hitler.

A brilliant intellect and a precise magician, Hitler was very specific in his actions. Having had his eye on the Spear of Longinus since he was a "starving artist" in Vienna, he could have acquired it almost anytime after he assumed power in Germany. But, he precisely waited until Austria was legally annexed whereupon he had papers drawn up to officially obtain possession of the spear by legal channels. His mystical visions told him that he must use the spear for evil. It was a harsh and deadly decision but it was his and he had to make it alone. It is somewhat like Christ making the decision for his own death. Here is Hitler, in the role of the Antichrist (Hitler's name commands more attention than any other villain in history), mimicking Christ. As was stated in *Montauk Revisited*, the role of the Christ and Antichrist are intimately related.

In the theater of planet Earth and the plotting of the gods, it was the Jewish situation that would ultimately undo Haushofer's grand plans. Haushofer had no primary interest in wiping out the Jews. As a matter of fact, he deeply appreciated their religion and his wife and son were part Jewish. I have even read one reference that he himself was one quarter Jewish. Regardless, Haushofer's own theory of Geopolitics dictated Aryan supremacy of the world. In fact, he was not the only high ranking Nazi to befriend the Jews. Hermann Goering, next in command if Hitler should die, was reportedly renowned for letting Jews out of the concentration camps as many of his officers were married to Jewish women. He was a soft touch and had no racial axe to grind, but he had to follow the political winds. Any of his efforts in this regard were permanently put to a stop when Heinrich Himmler complained to Hitler who gave Goering a terse order to restrain himself.

Haushofer was not only a brilliant man, he was reported to have used his clairvoyant ability for the war effort. He told Hitler when to invade Poland, when to invade France and nobody could believe how accurate his advice was. Everything went like clockwork and often against the advice of top Nazi generals who doubted Haushofer's advice from their own war room perspectives. Once Hitler began his conquest and started to feel his oats, the Final Solution got underway and this disgusted Haushofer to no end. He wanted to strip the Jews of the political power they retained in Germany, but he did not want a massacre. It was not part of his agenda and both the Thule and Vril societies saw that Hitler had become a wild card that could not be controlled.

By this time, Hitler was an absolute dictator and was not respectful of the societies that had put him into power. It is also entirely possible that some adepts in these societies silently approved because they knew exactly what was happening to Hitler. He was fulfilling his own personal destiny as the Antichrist.

On a conspiratorial and strategic level, probably no one felt more responsibility for the rise of Hitler than Karl Haushofer. He concocted a plan and contacted an old acquaintance who was very well known in magical circles in Germany. This person was Aleister Crowley. But, Haushofer couldn't just fly to England during war time. He used intelligence connections and Vatican passports and met with Ian Fleming in Lisbon, Portugal. Although Fleming is considerably more famous for authoring the James Bond novels, he was also a highly placed agent in M16 (the British equivalent of today's CIA). Haushofer sought the occult help of Crowley and told his plan to Fleming who also knew the master magician. Eventually, Haushofer made his way to England and met briefly with Crowley. What they decided would have a profound effect on the war.

The plan was to utilize Haushofer's old pupil, Rudolph Hess, to fly to Scotland and make peace with the British. This would stop the insane slaughter that was now out of hand. Hess was in awe of both Haushofer and Crowley and respected them both. Certain information was passed on to Hess from Crowley that were basically occult signals. At the same time, an extensive and elaborate magical ceremony was held in the Ashdown

Forest with plenty of military personnel on hand. Amado Crowley was in attendance (he is not the only source of this information) and Aleister conducted the ritual designed to bring Hess to Scotland.

In a feat of extraordinary aviation, Hess parachuted into Scotland and approached his old acquaintance, the Duke of Hamilton, in an effort to make peace between the warring nations. Churchill refused to meet with Hess and had no intention towards peace himself at that particular time. In fact, Gary Allen in *None Dare Call it Conspiracy* says that Churchill had a financial interest in certain armament factories in Germany which accordingly were not bombed.

Crowley had done his part, but it was not a small part. After that ceremony and Hess's departure, everything went haywire for the Nazis. Hitler was furious. Haushofer's influence was no longer magic. Astrologers and occultists were outlawed as Hitler now feared them. Hitler invaded Russia against everyone's advice and the war began to turn towards the Allies.

Haushofer's status was somewhat reduced after this episode but he was not without power. He planned an assasination attempt against Hitler that was to be physically carried out by his son Albrecht. The attempt failed and Albrecht was sentenced to be executed. He remained in prison for almost a year, wrote several sonnets and mused over his fate. Albrecht wondered why so many good people died in the war while Hitler survived only because someone had inadvertently moved a briefcase (which contained a bomb) at the last minute. Albrecht Haushofer realized before his own death that Hitler had to survive to carry out his role as the Antichrist. He said that people had to see the absolute horror that this man had generated, otherwise the world would never know and might let it happen again. Just before Hitler was reported to have died in the bunker, Heinrich Himmler ordered the execution of Albrecht Haushofer to be carried out. Himmler himself was escaping and was apparently afraid that Albrecht might implicate Himmler in the assasination attempt.

After the war, Karl Haushofer was the first occupant of what would eventually become known as the "Guest House". It was a large house in Nuremburg where "non dangerous Nazis" were put under light arrest. Haushofer testified at Nuremburg, primarily at the Rudolph Hess trial. Hess couldn't remember Haushofer nor any of the high ranking members of the Nazi Party. This fact is right in the regular history books and is not disputed. The Rudolph Hess that was tried at Nuremburg was either a double or a severely brainwashed individual. He was put in prison for life and was not allowed to talk about his Nazi past.

There are at least two accounts of Haushofer's death. One is that he committed hara-kiri, Japanese ritual suicide, on 14 March 1946. There is also a report from his interrogator, Father Edmund Walsh, that he died from arsenic poisoning on March 10, 1946. In addition to that, I have read a description of his death on March 9th when he and his wife took arsenic. Haushofer died but his wife didn't. She then hung herself over a creek. As his life was obscured by history, so was his death.

Edmund Walsh wrote a long article on Karl Haushofer in September of 1946 for *Life* magazine. He is not identified in the article as a reverend but as a military geopolitician. Walsh's account is suspect because he does not once touch upon Haushofer's occult background. Walsh is extremely condescending and morally righteous towards Haushofer, but he does relay a couple of points that are interesting.

At one point, Walsh sees to it that Haushofer is driven around the rubble of Nuremburg so that he can see the devastation that resulted from his theories. (Haushofer actually complained that his theories were misapplied by Hitler and the Nazi Party.) Walsh reports that Haushofer was very struck when the car stopped and he noticed a statue of a horse lying amidst the ruins of St. Egidien's Church. It commemorated Kaiser Wilhelm I, the founder of the German Empire. It was amazing that it hadn't gone down because everything else around it had been blown to bits. The following is a quote from the article:

"By one of those strange paradoxes that sometimes occur

during bombardments, this statue is intact and, though surrounded by rubble 10 feet deep at its base, the horseman is silhouetted against the sky and gazes imperiously over the wreckage of the Nazi empire. Haushofer stared at it for a long time without a syllable of comment. There was no necessity for me to embellish the symbolism".

Nuremburg was mentioned in *Montauk Revisited* as having been a sage radar sight for the U.S. Air Force. The symbology of the horse is bizarre. Duncan had always mentioned that the golden horse was in a city of ruins.

Walsh also reported another interesting thing about Haushofer. He said the man's last request was that his grave be unmarked. There are only two obvious reasons for this. Either Haushofer didn't want his grave to be desecrated or he didn't want anyone to know that he really wasn't dead. Haushofer was the head of an organization called Germans Abroad, and it was his job to see that German culture was exported all across the world. One thing is certain. The Thule and Vril societies went into hiding after the war. It is possible he may have joined them.

Karl Haushofer had a favorite saying. It was, "One who rides a tiger can't expect to get off." This was certainly an apt description of what his life became. When he did jump off the tiger, it was into the arms of Aleister Crowley, a man he thought could help him balance off the travesty that had been created.

There were many factors and causations that contributed to the war ending in the European theater, but it is undeniable that Crowley had waved his conductor's wand over the orchestra pit. In a magical sense, he had positioned himself so as to initiate the Nazi's fall from favor, all symbolized in a ritual that would over time become apparent as the Nazi's darkest hour.

23

IAN FLEMING AND
THE BRITISH CONNECTION

In the previous chapter it was mentioned that Karl Haushofer made his war time connection to Aleister Crowley through Ian Fleming. Fleming and Aleister Crowley were on very friendly terms. In fact, many circumstances in his novels were based either on Crowley's anecdotes or the grisly reputation he had acquired for himself. Fleming was also known to enjoy sex and the occult. It was even said that Agent 007 was an extension of his own personality. It is also possible that 007 designation may have been his actual coded identification.

In August of 1964, Ian Fleming was planning to fly to New Jersey and meet with another man in the British intelligence service: Ivan T. Sanderson. Sanderson was more famous as a radio personality and an explorer who had written several books. As a zoologist, he used to appear with animals on Johnny Carson's *Tonight Show*. Sanderson also embraced the paranormal and was probably the staunchest ally of Morris K. Jessup, the first man to attempt to find out the truth about the Philadelphia Experiment.

Al Bielek and Ivan Sanderson were friends during the 1960s and Al has an interesting memory concerning him. One day, Ivan startled Al by asking him about his brother Duncan. Al had no siblings in the Bielek family and didn't know what he was talking about. Ivan said they had all gone cave exploring together but the conversation was passed off as one of the many oddities that Al Bielek would accrue in his life. This was Al's first clue about his brother Duncan. Of course, Al would find his brother more than twenty years later.

Al has a clear memory of Sanderson's expected visit with Fleming. Key information concerning the Philadelphia Experiment was to be imparted to Sanderson and there was a strong anticipation that the mystery might finally be resolved. Then, on August 12th (the twenty-first anniversary of the Philadelphia Experiment), Fleming died of a sudden heart attack and the transfer of information did not take place.

Twenty-nine years later (astrologers will take note of the twenty-nine year cycle of Saturn), on August 12, 1993, I would receive a letter in my mail box from Amado Crowley confirming that his father had conducted a magical ritual on August 12, 1943, the same day as the Philadelphia Experiment. When I told Al about this occurrence, he was sure that a thirty year mystery had been solved — at least part of it. Fleming, in his opinion, was probably going to reveal some aspect of Crowley's knowledge as regards to the Rainbow Project. No one knows the whole story regarding Ian Fleming at this point, but the ritual described by Amado Crowley has provided major clues to the unraveling of Montauk. It reads as follows.

"On the 12th August, 1943, Aleister Crowley, myself, and five other people were gathered round an ancient stone monument, called Men-an-Tol, near Morvah in Cornwall, England. You will note the remarkable similarity of the name to Montauk. I enclose a photocopy of a postcard. The stone itself is called "a quoit" because it has a large circular hole in it. I was made to lie on a length of board, and this was inserted (me with it) into the hole. It was like the ferrite rod that is put into an electric coil. Aleister performed a ritual which appeared to "cause" a line of "rough water" between this spot in southern England, and Long Island in the USA."

As you will soon see, Amado was giving me a large piece of bait when he mentioned the similarity between the names of Men-an-Tol and Montauk.

24

MONTAUK DEFINED

It was Amado Crowley's clue regarding Men-an-Tol and Montauk which led me to the library (as discussed in Chapter Five) and unleashed the domino effect that has resulted in this book. Next, we will examine yet more deeply the definition of the word "Montauk".

Etymology, which is the study of word meanings and their origin, is an ancient tool of magicians and is considered by them to be a sacred science.* This tradition should be kept in mind as we examine the definition of the word "Montauk".

Montauk has several meanings. It has been defined by different authorities as "island place", "spirit", "spirit tree", "mount", "fortress" or "a place from which to observe". I have also spoken to a Taoist master on Long Island who is named Mantak Chia. He told me that the name "Mantak" was given to him and that it is a Tibetan word for "good virtue". In Tibetan, it also means clarity, understanding and bright light. In the *Webster's New World Dictionary*, virtue is derived from the Latin word *vir* which means man. The dictionary then refers

---

*It was common practice to reduce a sacred alphabet to numerical correspondences (A=1, B=2, etc.) and compare words that composed the same numbers. For example, the Greek word *agape* (love) has the same numerical equivalent as the Greek word *thelema* (will). In magick, these words are equivalent and one should love in accordance with one's will. They are, or should be, one and the same. This method is not as workable in English but correspondences will be found now and then.

us to the word "werewolf" which is derived from wei, to be strong or to have power. That the name "Mantak" should show up in Tibet is not too surprising because the Tibetan language has many words that are identical or similar to the Native American Hopi language. *Muyaw*, the Hopi word for sun is the Tibetan word for moon. *Tiawa*, the Hopi word for moon is the Tibetan word for sun. The Hopis speak Shoshone which is part of the Uto-Aztecan family of languages.

Native American shamans were also known to have spirit guides referred to as the "Manatu" or "Manitou". These were shape shifters and time travellers. The first syllable of their name relates to the Tibetan version of the word "mantak". If we relate the above definitions of this word, it translates as follows: mantak = virtue = man = power. In this sense, mantak would represent the total power or potential of man which would by the definition include shape shifting and time travelling.

According to J.J. Hurtak's glossary in the *Keys of Enoch*, "Tak" is the Tibetan word for Orion which is "a threshold of creation from our immediate physical galaxy into the next level of creation within our Father universe consisting of myriads of super super-galaxies." If we then add this definition of "tak" to the above meaning of "man", the meaning of "mantak" would be very similar. It is alluding to man's interdimensional nature.

If we pursue Hurtak's definition further, we are referred to Key 107. In verse 2, we are told that Orion is divided into at least two divisions. One is "star creation" referring to birth and regeneration. The other is "star death". He then says "Both are aligned with the Father's Throne governing through the star region of Alnitak, Alnilam, and Mintaka". Notice the similarity of the name "Mintaka" to Montauk. He goes on to say that Mintaka and the two other star regions are a "gateway which opens up our Son universe to the myriad star populations of our greater Father universe."

Of course, Tibetan is not the only language that gives a meaning for Montauk. According to one Gaelic linguist, Montauk and Men-an-Tol are both derived from the root *mer* which is associated with the sea but also means a circle of perpetual motion, like a vortex through which creation can manifest and from which one can conjure. *Mer* is also the root name of Merlin the magician which is derived from *mori* for sea and *dunn* for hill. This equates to sea hill or sea fortress. Note that Montauk has also been defined as a fortress by some Indian scholars. Sometimes *mar* is used instead of *mer* and this brings us back to the planet Mars, a planet that has often been thought of as having seas.

There is another intriguing etymology to Montauk if we consider the word "moon" which derives from *men* which means month or moon. *Men* not only relates to Men-an-Tol but also means blood. It is the root for menses which is the discharge of women during menstruation. The moon has always been the most valuable measure of time.

The word "Men-an-Tol" is derived from *men* which can also mean stone (derived from the Latin word *stipare*, to compress) or man and *tol* which means to take, tax, support or touch. In this sense, Men-an-Tol could mean to take man or to support man. One can go even further into this symbolism.

Perhaps the most important correspondence of the word "Montauk" can be found in its relationship with the word "Men-an-Tol". By this, I am referring to the temple of ancient Thebes known as the Temple of Mont or Montu. The Romans called it Mentu or Menthu. The first king of the first dynasty in Egypt was named Menes and he is believed to have laid the foundation for the first Temple of Montu as one of his first actions upon assuming power. Although this is legendary, whoever constructed the temple did so as homage to the war god Mars.

There are also words like "montology" which means the study of divination. "Mantle" or "manteau" refers to a cloak which was used for divination purposes. A priest's vestments are representative of this concept. There is also Montezuma, the Mexican Priest-King. His name actually translates out to Mohtecuzomatzin which means a brave and revered prince of noble birth. He played the role of Pharaoh for his people, quite unsuccessfully.

171

One could continue to keep adding to this list, but I'm sure you get the point. The only other one I'll mention is the Spanish word "montar". It means to ride horseback which is highly ironic when you consider that Duncan used to ride the golden horse that appears on the cover of *The Montauk Project*.

Upon reviewing all of the above definitions, it has occurred to me that I have spent countless hours researching this word as well as the phenomena of Montauk. It is therefore highly possible that I have become the world's foremost expert on the etymology of the word "Montauk". Accordingly, and with a bit of playfulness, I have defined it as follows:

Mon•tauk (mön′tôk′) [< Algonquin tribal name < Atlantean Vrillic *mon*, first, man, or first man (Adam) + *tok*, squeeze out, show, reveal. Word origin based upon earliest manifestation of man in the form of human consciousness extending into space time continuum and implied generation, degeneration and regeneration thereof. The word Montauk and its related phonemes are so closely tied to the original expression of thought that closely related words and sounds have arisen in various languages that mimic the original concept.] **1.** Colloquial name for an interdimensional gateway that is a conduit to the circulatory system of the planet and the higher forces of creation and sometimes manifests as vortices of energy that manifest near the eastern end of Long Island, New York, at various locations in the approximate vicinity of 71.4° Longitude, 41° Latitude. **2.** general name used to describe sacred Native American ground on eastern Long Island that was one time demarcated by pyramids and corresponds to an underlying energy body called the morphogenetic grid whereupon the Earth's consciousness and its entire physical constructs have manifested. **3.** name of a royal tribe of Native Americans who claim the name Pharoah and serve as the guardians of this grid. **4.** general reference to the Montauk Project or similar operations that seek to limit the consciousness of human beings and thereby prevent the full awakening of their human potential. **5.** a town on the eastern end of Long Island: pop. 12,666.

25

PRIEST OF MENTU

The definition of Montauk should make it easy to understand that we are dealing with the crossroads of a super highway of interdimensional information and sub quantum particles.
It is this exact super highway that magicians are trying to tap
into when they perform their magick. The purpose is generally
to access a portal, impart an intention and then have it bounce
back and manifest into the physical plane. In his storied career,
Aleister Crowley performed numerous magical acts and it was
his specific intention to contact as many entities and portals as
possible. Priest of Mentu (or Montauk) was one of the many
such titles he assumed in his work.

Crowley's role with Montauk is intrinsically connected
to the major magical work of his life: *The Book of the Law.*
This is a short but intensive work which has been interpreted
by many different scholars and magicians because it is considered to hold *the* major clue concerning magick. Extensive schol-
arship has been applied in this century in an attempt to unravel
this truth. In the next chapter, we will take a fresh new look at
this key.

First, in order to understand Crowley's Montauk connection, we must review how Crowley managed to run across *The
Book of the Law* in the first place. It begins with his marriage
to Rose Kelly on August 12, 1903. Rose was not into magick
or esotericism and was as "normal" a wife as Crowley ever

had, but if it wasn't for her, *The Book of the Law* wouldn't have happened. Consequently, their anniversary date is celebrated every year when the various lodges of the Ordo Templi Orientis hold a feast.

After their marriage, the Crowleys took a long trip to the orient. Upon their return, they realized it was advisable to remain in the lower latitudes so as to avoid the cold February weather in England. As a result, and at the last minute, they decided to visit the city of Mars: Cairo, Egypt. It wasn't long before Crowley took his wife to the Great Pyramid where they spent an evening in the King's Chamber. There they were: young newlyweds in the midst of Tahuti, the dweller on the threshold.

The entire experience had a profound effect on Rose. When they returned to their flat in Cairo, she fell into an altered state of consciousness. This was very odd for her as she was not an occultist of any sort. In her trance, she kept repeating that Crowley had offended Horus, the Egyptian god. Crowley was quite astonished as Rose knew virtually nothing about Egyptian mythology. She proceeded to tell him how to invoke Horus and soon dragged him to the Boulak Museum. There, his astonishment turned to shock. She showed him an image of Horus in a form known as Ra-Hoor-Khuit. The image was contained in a stone monument which is known as the Stele (which means inscribed stone or slab) of Ankh-af-na-khonsu, also identified as the Priest of Menthu. The stele's museum display number was "666" which was the number Crowley identified himself with. This experience would not only change Crowley's life forever, it arguably initiated the key magical events of this yuga, including the Babalon Working (which Jack Parsons believed to be the fourth book of *The Book of the Law* — Crowley's work consisted of three books).

At midnight on March 19th*, Crowley declared that the

---

* March 18th is the traditional birth date of Christ according to the esoteric tradition. It also represents the sun moving from the constellation Pisces (ruled by Neptune which represents illusion) into that of Aries (ruled by Mars which represents reality and the fire of war amongst many other things).

Equinox of the Gods had arrived and a new epoch in human history had begun. On April 8, 9 and 10th of the year 1904 he dictated a message from Aiwass whom he identified as his own guardian angel. Aiwass was to serve as a link between the solar spiritual forces and mankind. The message became known as *The Book of the Law* and laid down a simple code of conduct which is "Do what thou wilt shall be the whole of the law. Love is the law, love under will. There is no law beyond Do what thou wilt." Never was this law meant to "do anything you feel like". It means to carry out your true purpose as defined by the circumstances of the universe, yourself and all of creation. It is important to note that *The Book of the Law* has been subject to incredible misinterpretation.*

Before Crowley came along, the Stele of Ankh-af-na-khonsu was primarily known only as "Stele 666". He called it the "Stele of Revealing" which is how it is commonly referred to by occultists today. The revelation has to do with information that is imparted through Crowley in *The Book of the Law*. A review of this book and the original stele will show that one feeds off the other. In some respects, *The Book of the Law* could be called a translation but an expounding of certain principles would be a more apt description.

The revelation has to do with the hawk-headed god Horus who is the Egyptian equivalent of the Roman god Mars. The Egyptian pantheon was much more flexible and "multi-personaed" than that of the Greeks or Romans, and many of the gods had subtle and multiple aspects. In fact, Horus is splintered into many of the different deities that appear in *The Book of the Law*. Aiwass, the being who is dictating the book to Crowley, is an aspect of Horus and reveals himself as "the inspired forth-speaker of Mentu". Mentu is a form of Horus with respect to the planet Mars. Ankh-af-na-khonsu is a form Horus with respect to the moon.

The Book of the Law clearly designates Crowley as the

---

* Anyone interested in reading *The Book of the Law* should start with Crowley's *The Law Is For All*. It gives the text of the original work plus two interpretations that Crowley wrote at different periods of his life.

Prophet of Mentu or Priest of Mentu. By following the various etymologies given in this book, one can see that Crowley could be aptly described as a prophet or priest of both Mars and Montauk.

Consistently during the book, Horus identifies himself as a warrior and god of war. He says:

"3. Now let it be first understood that I am a god of War and of Vengeance. I shall deal hardly with them. 4. Choose ye an island! 5. Fortify it! 6. Dung it about with enginery of war! 7. I will give you a war-engine. 8. With it ye shall smite the peoples; and none shall stand before you."

Crowley first interpreted the above passage about the island to refer to a chakra of the human spiritual system. He later implied the island was England and that the matter was a military secret. Then, he says that the English war-engine is probably a foreshadowing of a Great War where Horus shall triumph utterly.

Keeping in mind that Montauk is geologically an island and was once known as such, the implications of the above passage are quite unmistakable. This is especially true if you consider that the German secret societies (Vril and Thule) had extensive contacts in the OTO and probably studied *The Book of the Law* in addition to similar documents that have yet to see the light of day. This could explain at least part of the fascinations the Germans have had with Montauk as a strategic point.

An additional correspondence is found in Crowley's chosen name of Aleister (his parents named him Edward Alexander) because it is derived from a Greek word for the god of vengeance. He selected the name long before he ever put *The Book of the Law* together and wrote the phrase "I am a god of War and Vengeance".

After the above revelation about choosing an island, Aiwass (who equates to Horus and Crowley) says "I am the warrior Lord of the Forties: the Eighties cower before me, and are abased. I will bring you to victory and joy: I will be at your arms in battle and ye shall delight to slay. Success is your proof;

courage is your armour; go on, go on, in my strength; and ye shall turn not back for any!"

The reference to the 1940s and 1980s is unmistakable. The Forties opened a time door with the Philadelphia Experiment. World War II has sometimes been referred to as a war of time. Victory and joy would at first refer simply to the World War II victory, but this is not the case. The Eighties were abased with reference to the disaster at Montauk that climaxed in 1983, but victory and joy are at hand on a larger scale particularly if we consider the coming age of enlightenment in regards to the yugas.

Crowley himself interprets this passage in a different fashion then says, "I am inclined to opine that there is a simpler and deeper sense in the text than I have so far disclosed."

There is indeed a deeper sense and it begins to be understood when we recognize Crowley's involvement with the intelligence and military communities, part of which has already been discussed. His magical influence is clearly seen when we consider that his secret name within the OTO was Phoenix. The Phoenix Project was, of course, the code name for Montauk and for all similarly related projects. Almost anything in the military industrial complex which was a secret project was labeled "Phoenix".

In Egyptian mythology, the phoenix was a big bird that erected its own funeral pyre every 666 (or 500 depending on which version you read) years and would renew itself by rising from the ashes as a completely new bird. The phoenix was represented by a heron or hawk as a vehicle of the god Horus whose messenger, Aiwass, communicated *The Book of the Law*. The god Horus gives another amazing correspondence when we realize that the word "hero" is derived from the word "Horus". The Montauk Air Force Station is called Camp Hero. Horus is also the root for the word "horology" which is defined as the art of measuring time or making clocks. In this sense Camp Hero means "Camp of Time Measurement".

As for what "Phoenix" did while he was at Montauk, Amado Crowley has provided some clues. According to

Amado's account, Crowley went there with a specific intention. He wasn't dabbling with new experiments nor with any of the rituals his secret societies keep so proudly cloistered. He was setting up a certain type of "receiver". This was done across the planet at other strategic sites as well. The ritual at Men-an-Tol on August 12, 1943 was "making an emission". He was told by his father that a certain type of "energy" would excite a network of similar sites to come into being for a certain period of time. Although the geological theory of the day did not include the idea of "tectonic plates", Amado says that this network of energy sites very closely coincided with the faults in the earth's crust. (There is a major fault off Montauk Point which has been popularized in a fiction novel entitled *The Montauk Fault* by Robert Mitgang.)

Asking his father if he wanted to set off volcanoes or trigger earthquakes, Crowley replied, "Nothing as simple as that!"

In other words, it was a complex operation. As a youngster, Amado believed they were "fighting the baddies" and thereby thwarting the plans of another group. If things were really that complex, they must have been so for a considerable period of time. This implies that there would have been practical applications for regulating the grid with technological hardware for doing it. Consequently, Amado believes that Crowley was spying on the other group in addition to doing real occult work.

Who was the other group? No one seems to be quite sure at this point. The Germans are implied but it also points to the alien connection at Montauk. We will examine that shortly but first, we will examine the key to Crowley's *The Book of the Law*.

26

THE BOOK OF THE LAW

As was stated in the last chapter, *The Book of the Law* is thought by many to contain THE secret as regards magick. Anyone who studies it seriously will learn that the work is rich with numerical correspondences that are being directed from a higher source. It is far too complex a piece of writing to have been concocted by a scheming human mind. As for the secret to the book itself, it is referred to in Part III, verse 47:

"This book shall be translated into all tongues: but always with the original in the writing of the Beast; for in the chance shape of the letters and their position to one another: in these are mysteries that no Beast shall divine. Let him not seek to try: but one cometh after him, whence I say not, who shall discover the Key of it all. Then this line drawn is a key: then this circle squared in its failure is a key also. And Abrahadabra. It shall be his child and that strangely. Let him not seek after this; for thereby alone can he fall from it."

The Book of the Law has been published in various formats but according to the book itself, there is only one format that is correct: a red cover with golden letters. It is further stipulated that a replication of Crowley's original handwritten manuscript must be included in the book. Why? If one looks at page sixteen of the handwritten manuscript, a grid has been laid out against the above quotation. It has been reproduced on page 181. It is more than a curiosity to me as to why those who write or comment on *The Book of the Law* never even point out that this grid pattern exists, let alone try and interpret it. If one just reads the typeset version that is published, one misses the entire meaning. I will now share what I have discovered regarding this cryptic secret.

The most obvious visual on the page is that the idea of a grid is suggested along with the line drawn across Crowley's handwriting. If one puts a protractor against the line, one notices that it inclines at a 26° angle. This is an interesting geometrical relationship because it represents the angles of at least two major passageways in the Great Pyramid. First is the descending passageway that leads to the "Chamber of Chaos" as it is sometimes called. Second, is the ascending passageway that leads to the Grand Gallery and also to the Queen's Chamber. The latter contains a shaft which would let the light shine in from the star Sirius just prior to the rainy season and heralded the beginning of the year. Sirius corresponds to this 26° angle because in ancient times it rose on the horizon 26.5° south of due east. The sun itself rose 26.5° north of due east. Further, I have been told that if you lay out the 26° angle of the ascending passage in the Great Pyramid on a flat plane that it will point straight to Jerusalem. This line gives us a key to walk into the Great Pyramid itself. This is, of course, where Crowley and his wife spent the night prior to receiving *The Book of the Law*.

My next attempt to understand this puzzle was to connect all the letters that the above line touched as per the line "for in the chance shape of the letters and their position to one another: in these are mysteries that no Beast shall divine". If you connect the letters that the line goes through, you get the following: S, T, B, E, T, I, S, A, Y, F, A. Rearranging these letters, it spells out the following: EASY IF BAST or IF BAST EASY. I soon discovered that Bast is an obscure goddess in the Egyptian pantheon but is also considered to be another expression or spelling for "The Beast". Information about this goddess is hard to find and I'm told it has been deliberately hidden. She does correspond to the star Sirius mentioned above,

16

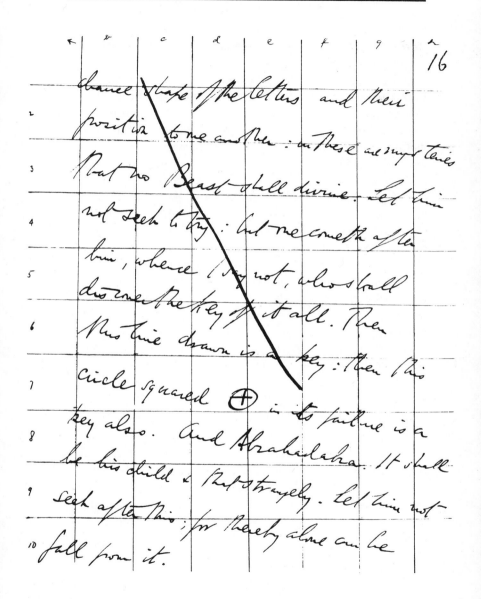

channel shape of the letters and their
position to one another: in these are mysteries
that no Beast shall divine. Let him
not seek to try: but one cometh after
him, whence I say not, who shall
discover the Key of it all. Then
this line drawn is a key: then this
circle squared ⊕ in its failure is a
key also. And Abrahadabra. It shall
be his child & that strangely. Let him not
seek after this; for thereby alone can he
fall from it.

but we'll discuss that a bit later.

Attempting to verify what I had found, I took this to an occult cryptologist I know who sometimes does psychic work for the police. He loves puzzles and welcomed the challenge. I faxed him Crowley's handwriting, and he became very concerned. As he is also a graphologist (one who interprets personality traits based upon handwriting), he asked if it was my handwriting. I told him no. He said that was good because if it was we could no longer be friends. I asked him why, and he informed me that whoever wrote it was a sadist, a masochist, an extreme pessimist with definite sexual problems but also a genius who had <u>incredible</u> occult knowledge. I told him it was Crowley's handwriting and he laughed. The cryptologist told me that the correspondence to Bast made sense but that I should also try connecting the words that the line runs through and not just the letters. The words that are connected are as follows: SHAPE, TO, BE, TRY, I, SAY, and A. Note that I have only used words that are composed of letters that are within the confines of the squares on the grid. This translates to: I SAY TRY TO BE A SHAPE or I SAY TRY A SHAPE TO BE. or I TRY TO SAY BE A SHAPE. If one wishes to extend the word "be" into "Beast" and/or add the word "of", one gets this: I SAY TRY TO SHAPE A BEAST or I TRY TO SAY SHAPE OF A BEAST or I SAY TO TRY SHAPE OF A BEAST.

The clearest of these phrases is "I try to say be a shape" and is more correct according to the cryptologist and the rules of cryptograms. I have added the others because they all reduce to a common denominator as you will soon see.

The next clue to understanding what Crowley is talking about is in the symbol drawn within square d-7. It is also known as the Mark of the Beast:

Crowley's writings says "Then this line drawn is a key: then this circle squared ⊕ in its failure is a key also." There are at least two ways to interpret this that make sense to me. First, Crowley was trained in traditional mathematics. In school, his teachers would have fed him the paradox that if given a compass and a straight edge (with no marks of measure), one cannot make a square that will be equal to the area of the circle. To this day, this is still the rule in modern math. But, Crowley says "in its failure is a key also". The definition of the word "failure" includes "neglect or omission".

In this respect, squaring the circle is a two dimensional operation. If you extend this procedure into three dimensions, you can cube a sphere through the unfolding of the Platonic solids that was discussed previously. With a 3D pencil that writes in thin air, one could conceivably accomplish the task.

If we then apply three dimensions to the Mark of the Beast or the cross within the circle, we get a very interesting configuration. First, we will connect the end points of the cross in order to obtain the following two dimensional design:

Although illustrated in two dimensions, this is a representation of a three dimensional octahedron within a sphere. In order to visualize this, you need to consider that you are looking down on an octahedron within a sphere. If this is not clear, it will help to imagine putting your fingers from both hands at the center of the cross and pulling it upward with one hand and downward with the other. The result is an octahedron with the circle translating into a three dimensional sphere. If none of this is clear, construct an octahedron out of sticks and look at it from the top. It will look like a cross.

The octahedron is not only a sacred shape, it is the Delta-T antenna that was so crucial to the time experiments used at

183

Montauk. It is also the design of the Great Pyramid itself. As was stated in earlier chapters, the octahedron can be derived from symmetrical tetrahedrons as can the square, icosahedron and dodecahedron. Because the five platonic solids can in turn be used to simulate any design in nature, this design is representative of the key to the morphogenetic grid and to life itself.

When we are told, "try to be a shape" or "be a shape", it is a direct inference to the geometric fields that are layered within the electromagnetic structure of our entire make up. If one can visualize these various shapes, one is getting down to the core of one's entire being or matrix structure as it is sometimes called. It is the key to referencing oneself amidst the vast panorama of creation. What has already been said about sacred geometry should clearly indicate that a doorway is opened by addressing these principles. Of course, if the words are extended to mean "try to be a beast shape" or "try to be of a beast shape", we are facing the same principle. The animal world, including the human body, is made of geometric shapes.

As I said earlier, there is another way to interpret this passage. In this regard, it should be pointed out that the idea of the circle squared in traditional mathematics is entirely arbitrary. A mathematician told me that this phrase could have other legitimate meanings. For example, it can also refer to the fact that you can derive a square from a circle by cutting its circumference four times with its radius. This gives you the first glyph illustrated in this chapter. One can then make the square by connecting the four points where the radii intersect with the circumference. This gives us the second glyph. Applying three dimensions, we obtain the Delta-T antenna and the unfolding of the Platonic solids. But, *The Book of the Law* states "in its failure is a key also". This requires a different approach from what was meant in the previous definition of failure. This can perhaps be understood by studying the "one who cometh after him who shall discover the key of it all".

Crowley and many others believed this man was Charles Stansfield Jones, a magician who died years ago. He was Crowley's magical son and had shown much promise. I have

184

seen an artistic representation of Jones' insight which was an unfoldment of geometric patterns just as we discussed. There was no explanation accompanying it. In itself, it would not provide any sort of clue to the uninformed. It does indicate that Jones had tremendous insight. He also wrote an unpublished book entitled Liber XXXI. Although I haven't seen it, I don't suspect he mentioned the geometry referred to here, but he did grasp it. That is for sure. There was only one problem: he was insane.

After a storied magical career, Jones took "the Oath of the Abyss". This essentially means that he interpreted every single event in his life as having magical significance. He had a great intellect and a wealth of magical knowledge but it all got the better of him. After having gone to England to join the Roman Catholic Church in an unsuccessful attempt to convert them to the Law of Thelema, he returned home via ship to Vancouver and disembarked wearing only a raincoat. He soon cast it aside and did a ritual around the center of the city in an attempt to free himself from all restriction. As one can easily imagine, he was summarily arrested and made the butt of many jokes in jail. Jones had dramatic insight but had failed as a human being in that he could not integrate his knowledge with this reality. He ended up having magical wars with Crowley and declared him an enemy. If this man had discovered "the key", why did he end up in such a ludicrous position?

My own brief study of Jones tells me that he was extremely majestic and wrapped up in the flamboyance of what he could accomplish as a magician. Further, he was incredibly lacking in common sense. Crowley said that he had skipped grades in his magical order and had suffered the consequences. The man obviously had incredible insights and pursued them to the detriment of his own evolution. He was putting his intellectual accomplishment ahead of his heart.

With respect to this second interpretation, it doesn't matter if Jones failure (despite his enlightenment) was being referred to by Crowley or not. The geometric evidence is clear, but we have to learn from his failure.

Anyone who receives information of this sort is propelled into a state of wonder. It leaves one with the feeling that maybe they should spend their lives studying the Great Pyramid and the tenets of the various mystery schools. It is all quite fascinating and it's easy for us to be seduced by the incredible complexity of nature and sacred geometry. If we understand it very well, we can even seduce others. But, if one does not follow the path of the human heart, there will be extreme failure.

The human heart could also be termed the divine spark. It is the very facility that the Pharaoh used as he interfaced with both the higher and lower energies. Its absence results in decay which is the malady of our present world. "Let him not seek after this; for thereby alone can he fall from it" suggests that we should not become obsessed with pursuing any of this information. If it comes to us, fine. It is fascinating information, but neither the intricacies of creation, UFOs, abductions, or Montauk and the like should become obsessions. We must keep our balance.

There is a lot more that could be said about *The Book of the Law*. It could warrant another book and another year of study, but none of that is within the editorial guidelines of this work. I have tried to present a view of the book that I have not seen written previously. More importantly, it corresponds to Montauk and the rest of the information herein. It is important to remember that the only value *The Book of the Law* has is as a key to consciousness. If it opens doors to your understanding, then you have found THE key. If THE key doesn't answer all of life's questions, you will find that the book will recycle and give you another key. It is simply a tool by which you can approach and grasp your own connection with the infinite.

27

THE SIRIANS

The most important aspect concerning the discoveries made in the previous chapter is that they explain key aspects of our ancient heritage. As was already said, *The Book of the Law* leads us into the Great Pyramid with a line drawn at a 26° angle. We are also led to the Sphinx when the anagram of Bast appears in the book. This leaves us in the middle of two ancient wonders and right next to Cairo, the city of Mars. It has already been demonstrated that Egypt as well as many other aspects of our civilization have fashioned themselves to serve as a tribute to the planet Mars, but there was another heavenly body that was held in even higher regard: the star Sirius.

Shining as the brightest star in our heavens, the Egyptians based their entire calendar on the movement of this sacred star. It was already indicated that he Great Pyramid was built to synchronize with Sirius so that the star would shine through the hole to the Queen's Chamber at a precise moment. Esoteric writings indicate that the light shining through the shaft was meant to impart the starlight of Sirius to an initiate during a ritual. If Egypt was so fascinated with Sirius, it stands to reason that the ancient civilization of Mars had a similar reverence for the star. In fact, the geometric shapes on the planet Mars have been said to be built in tribute to Sirius.

According to one legend, the face on Mars was in honor of the god or solar logos known as Sukon. The Sirians settled

Mars through his permission. He has also been identified as Set or Seth. The reason the Sirians settled Mars was because it was at that time in the cradle orbit of life. Taking 720 days to get around the sun would have resulted in the most preferable weather that was conducive to civilization at that particular time period.

In *The Montauk Project*, it was the Sirians who provided the Montauk chair used for the time experiments. It was a Mr. X who had approached me and told me that he had been involved in negotiations to obtain the chair. This man also told me of Crowley's ability to manipulate time and was the first to suggest that the Philadelphia Experiment and Montauk Project were both resulting effects of Crowley's magick.

All of this is very ironic when one looks yet deeper into Crowley's secret connections. Crowley was not only involved in the OTO but was also a member of an arcane secret society known as the A∴ A∴ (Argenteum Astrum) or the Order of the Silver Star. The "silver star" referred to is Sirius itself, the most prominent in the heavens and positioned as the chief star in the ancient constellation "Phoenix". The ancient Assyrians and Phoenicians both derive their name from this legacy.

Crowley identified the Order of the Silver Star as the Illuminati itself. As he was considered to be the head of the Illuminati, the correspondences continue to run even deeper. The heart of his magical current was inspired from Sirius and there was much tradition to back this up. In occult tradition, Sirius is the Hidden God or "the sun behind the sun". As the moon reflects the sun, so does the sun reflect Sirius. This concept was expressed in *The Book of the Law* when Crowley wrote "The Khabs is in the Khu, not the Khu is in the Khabs." The word Khab means star while Khu refers to light. What is being taught here is that collective "wisdom" often assumes that the stars emanate light. The truth of the matter is that the stars are in the light and are merely reflecting it. It was in this sense that Crowley and the ancients who worshipped Sirius were worshiping the light of creation. Sirius was the brightest star, therefore it reflected the most light and was the most powerful.

188

According to the ancient Egyptians, there was a special occult link between Sirius and the Earth when they were at their closest distance. In other words, more universal light was being reflected from Sirius that at any other time of the year. This link was found to be most powerful during the Dog Days of August (Sirius is known as the Dog Star) which run from July 23rd to August 23rd. Some consider them to peak out as late as September 8th. This aspect of Sirius is very synchronistic if you remember the theory referred to in *The Montauk Project* that the biorhythms of the Earth run every twenty years on August 12th. This date is not only the anniversary of Crowley's wedding, the Philadelphia Experiment and the culmination of the Montauk Project; it is right in the center of the Dog Days. Of course, the Montauk chair was supposed to be supplied by the Sirians. Obviously, if this whole incredible Montauk scenario is true, it stands to reason that the Sirians might have an idea or two about how to make a chair that resonates with the consciousness of time.

According to information from the Montauk story, the Sirians were technical creatures and were not very political. According to Al Bielek, the Sirians look very human in some respects. They are muscular but have vertical slit eyes, like a cat's eyes. They wear a covering over their hair, and it is suspected that they are bald. Sometimes they have strange things on their ears which could be communicating devices. They are approximately six feet in height and can pass for humans in the proper attire. At Montauk, they were generally affable and did their job.

Not too much else has been said about them, nor do I have anything more to add from that quarter. What is important is that they seem to have a rather strong correspondence in the information that is being revealed.

A book entitled *The Twelfth Planet* by Zacharia Sitchin documents very well that Earth has been visited by extraterrestrial critters since time immemorial. This work traces the activity back to ancient Sumeria which is exactly where the Sirians settled. All of this not only places the Sirians at the focal point of our planetary theology, it makes them a center of all sorts of alien activity.

Crowley studied this time line at its source when he examined the ceremonial rites of the Sirians or ancient Sumerians, whatever you want to call them. In history, these beings were known as the shepherd kings and they were called the Yezidi. Their prophet was Yezid and Crowley discovered that he was a reincarnation of him.

As Crowley studied these ancient Sumerians and their rites, he learned they were sexual in the extreme and orgiastic. The ceremonies were all done in synchronization with the stellar revolutions. Many eventually found their way into the Roman and Greek mystery schools. These ancients looked at the primitive urges in a much different way that "civilized" society does today. Not unlike animals in mating season, they recognized instinctually that revolutions of the universe coincided with sexual urges that enabled one to gain access to invisible worlds or other dimensions. In the Hindu tantric arts which is known as the yoga of love, these urges would be better defined as kalas which are units of time or vaginal vibrations. If one reduces space and time to its male and female aspects, it is easy to grasp that Mother Nature is going to have undulations that correspond to the vagina. Earlier in this book, the vesica pisces was illustrated. This was an eye shaped glyph that resulted as the second act of creation unfolded. It is not only the shape of an eye, it is known as the Eye of Horus or as the Eye of Set (Sirius). When this "eye" is in a vertical position, it is symbolic of the vagina.

As the geometry of space and time unfolds in the evolutionary process (which is known as Mother Nature), there are processes and repetitions that mimic or harmonize with what we know as the sexual process. These very energies are incredibly powerful as they make creation a reality. Of course, the morphogenetic grid is the blueprint that becomes reality. It is in this manner that the ancient Sumerians or Sirians did orgiastic rites. They were honoring the undulations and unfoldments of geometric evolution by linking their consciousness through the sexual process.

We all know that we go into a different state of consciousness during the sexual act. As it is a creational process, it is not hard to relate that we can then have an effect on creation when in this form of consciousness. When we engage in sex, we are tapping into the blueprint that made the whole universe possible.

As Crowley studied this information, he saw that the ancients understood what they were doing in their orgiastic rites. Of course, if you were to walk in on an orgy today, you might find that the procedure has degenerated into an unholy mess. On the other hand, magical energies would definitely be present.

All of this brings us back to Bast*, the goddes of witchcraft and sexual magick in the Egyptian pantheon. If you ever had the urge to do anything of a bizarre sexual nature, you were entering the realm of Bast. Who exactly was she?

Often identified as the Egyptian cat goddess, Bast is one of the most ancient forms of Babalon, the Mother goddess. Bast is portrayed as both a cat and lion. As the goddess of

---

* In Chapter 26, I referred to the line drawn in *The Book of the Law* as forming the phrase "EASY IF BAST". Upon reading the first draft of this manuscript, one of my friends took strong issue with this correspondence and sarcastically said why didn't I pick "EASY IF STAB". She was refuting that I had come up with a meaningful correspondence. I knew that Bast wasn't the whole key but it did yield a lot of insightful information. The next day, I met an author who offered me all sorts of information on Jack the Ripper. To my surprise, I realized that there was a host of meaning to "EASY IF STAB" if one approached it from a study of Jack the Ripper. Not only is there a whole body of data regarding Aleister Crowley and Jack the Ripper, Crowley was rumored to have known his identity. If one considers that the name "Jack" is synchronistic with Jack Parsons, it gives one more pause to wonder. I have not had the time to research this, but I am sure we could find some very interesting correspondences between Jack the Ripper by approaching *The Book of the Law* through "EASY IF STAB". The mystery of Jack the Ripper's identity was never solved. My intuition tells me that he was an interdimensional creature of some sort. That he killed prostitutes is only a further correspondence to Crowley. It has also been said that the mystery schools protect the energies of the Great Pyramid because if they are accessed, one can destroy anything one wants without being traced. If one considers this aspect of the pyramid and compares the killings of Jack the Ripper to cattle mutilations (in order to access vital glands and organs) by aliens, it offers many intriguing possibilities for investigation.

sexual magick, she ruled over lust and sexual heat. It was her job to see that all potentialities manifested and had their day in the sun. Bast is readily identified as the Beast because she "presided" over the vast sexual experiments of Atlantis (and later Egypt) which gave rise to mermaids, minotaurs, centaurs, Pegasus and the like.

Bast's legacy gives us at least two words in our modern lexicon. The word "bastard" was derived from the Pandora's Box that opened with the unrestricted breeding practices that were common during her reign. During the reign of the goddess, paternity was not an issue. Marriage came into being in large part due to the need to preserve a patriarchal structure for inheritance and succession purposes. When the father god took over, he made parentage an issue and punished women who bore children outside of the established tradition of wedlock. This is not so much a moral issue as a power issue.

Amazon cultures were known to be able to breed without the use of a male. Because the human body is primarily androgynous, a separation of the sexes is not theoretically necessary for procreation. This contention about the Amazons is backed up by the fact that the zona pellucida (the reproductive body in the female which contains a sack) can be penetrated by a latent male protein within the inherited genetic structure of the female that the body thinks and treats like a sperm. This results in a virgin birth.

It could be argued that the Amazons were unbalanced in the direction of the female energies. Whether or not that is true is not the point. Their culture and the general goddess culture of that time period was supplanted by a patriarchal culture that has attempted to subjugate women to the most unbearable of conditions. The male forces established control. Morality was then generated by the power elite of that particular civilization.

On a very primal level, the purpose of the female energies is to regenerate through the sexual organs. This is the gateway to immortality for the beast or animal form of the species. Only through the female genitalia can the beast project its im-

age into a future circumstance and thus obtain perpetual life for his/her kind. Bast symbolized this and also the idea of uninhibited breeding practices which is sometimes known as "catting". This is the derivation of the word "cunt", common slang for the vagina but almost always used in a derogative sense. This word is so taboo that it has earned its way onto the "list of seven dirty words" that cannot be used on television or radio. As you can see, Bast's influence has no small part in our culture. One can easily see that the rancor and enmity that generally accompanies the words "bastard" and "cunt" derives from the ancient criticism of the culture that was prevalent during the time of Bast.

Crowley's concept of the Scarlet Woman or Babalon is another name for the goddess Bast. Scarlet is chosen because it is the color of blood (also the color chosen for the cover of *The Book of the Law*). As stated earlier, blood represents the passage of the moon and the menstrual period. The lunar calendar is therefore the calendar of Bast and represents the true time line. This is in direct opposition to the Gregorian calendar that was given to us by the decree of Pope Gregory, the same pope who authorized the inquisition.

In regard to her lunar aspect, Bast's offspring were known as children of the moon, hence the name moon child. In the previous chapter, Crowley was identified as the incarnation of the Priest Ankh-af-an-Khonsu which equates to the Priest of Mentu. As Khonsu also refers specifically to the moon, Bast can be identified as the Priestess of Mentu with regard to her lunar aspect. It is in this respect that Bast could be considered to have presided over the sexual and genetic experiments that are said to have occurred at Montauk. In what is an amusing correspondence, there are usually various cats that roam the picnic area near the lighthouse parking lot at Montauk. They have no apparent home but are always well fed by the tourists who sometimes take one home for a pet. These cats are known as the "Montauk Cats". I was once told that if you follow the cats before a rainstorm, they will lead you to the underground.

Although Bast's correspondence with Montauk is a bit

obscure, Bast was glorified in ancient Egypt as the Sphinx. She had the loins of a lion, symbolized by the constellation Leo and the top half of a virgin woman, symbolized by the constellation Virgo. The Sphinx had breasts at one point, but these were defaced as the patriarchal culture established its foothold. The face was also altered at one point to look more like a chimpanzee. This desecration of the Sphinx prompts an important question: why did we get a chimp?

The answer lies in our genetics. Human evolution on this planet has been primarily restricted to the biology of the ape. It was said previously in this book that Rh positive blood refers to the rhesus monkey genetics being present in the human system. Rh negative implies an alien blood type. One can also see a resemblance to apes in human beings. If you don't believe me, just go to the gorilla exhibit at the zoo.

The word "monkey" itself gives us an interesting play on words. "Mon" refers to Montu, Montauk or the earlier definitions provided for that phoneme while "key" refers to the "key to Montauk". Although there is some contention about it amongst scholars, "Monkey" derives from the Dutch word *monnekijn* which traces back to the Roman word *monne*, the origin of which is uncertain. The handwriting is on the wall. *Manikan* means little man or an imitation of man. *Monne* is intimately related to the root words already covered.

The word "ape" is said to be borrowed from a Teutonic word yet there is argument and some say it is really from the Celts. It all becomes clear when we consult the derivition of the word "apex". This means several interesting things. It is the highest culminating point of time and also refers to the vertex of a triangle or the conical top of a pyramid. Apex strongly suggests the concept of the Tower of Babalon or the mountain aspect of Montauk. The word itself derives from tip, specifically referring to the tip of a flamen's cap. (A flamen was a priest or magician in ancient Rome, the word deriving from the Sanskrit word *brahman*.)

Orangutan derives from *oran* which means man and *utan* which equates to forest. The word *oran* is a Malaysian word which is suspiciously close to Orion. Chimpanzee derives from "pan" which means all embracing. It also refers to Pan, the god of the forest and fields. He was quite sexually active and Crowley wrote a lot of poetry about him.

Gorilla was coined as a word by the real life Doc Savage based upon a West African word for a race of hairy women. It is a direct reference to a genetic specimen that we don't see or hear too much about today. You can read the book *Mother was a Lovely Beast* by Philip José Farmer for more information along this line.

The point of all this is very clear and the phrase "to monkey around with" takes on a whole new meaning. Somebody monkeyed with our genetics in quite a literal sense. In the time of Bast, all types of genetic samplings were embraced. The conquering influence chose to propagate a similitude with the apes through the morphogenetic grid of evolution.

Bast established that human consciousness could become a lower form it if chose to or that the lower forms could obtain the equivalent of human consciousness. This is a sacrilegious teaching to many, but it was highly regarded as the truth in times past. The city of Bubastis was found by archeologists to contain a multitude of mummified cats who stood as guardians of the temple. The reverence to Bast was intense.

The Book of the Law teaches us that the propagation of life is completely unrestrictive in its nature. All potentialities are real and this is accomplished through the evolving geometries that lie beneath the blue print of evolution. The goddess Bast champions the unrestricted potential of all creation. Our limitations in evolution are influenced by those who dominate the morphogenetic grid but are essentially determined by our own free will and choice in the matter.

28

IS A GOD TO LIVE IN A DOG?

The desecration of Bast in our culture makes the ancient Sumerian sexual rites very taboo. One can readily see this in the mores of mainstream Christianity that permeate our entire culture. The Sumerians looked at life from a totally opposite view. In their sex rites, they believed they were honoring the light or the electromagnetic spectrum of creation that manifests in the various heavenly bodies of the galaxy. The light was all of creation and the sexual process was what joined god and beast. The concept of the Holy Trinity was used to sell the idea that God created man through spirit alone. While this is not altogether untrue, it was preached in such a manner to divide man from beast. This is a prime example of polarized thought. It is quite divisive.

What is peculiarly ironic is that throughout the years, the Church has insisted on the doctrine of Jesus having a virgin birth. Practitioners of magick, who are often enemies of Church doctrine, have no problem with that idea whatsoever. Where they differ is that they will not hold man to be totally separate from the beast. There are many reasons for this and one is particularly academic. It has to do with Jehovah.

In an earlier chapter we clarified that Jehovah's name in Hebrew is JHVH or YHWH or IHVH. This stands for the four Hebrew letters Yod, Hé, Vod, and Hé. What I did not tell you is that if you transpose the letters IHVH to HIVH, you have the Hebrew word for beast which is pronounced *heva*. As this word has the same numerological equivalent to Jehovah, they are considered to be one and the same. It is the pure magick of the alphabet. Actually, both words add up to the number "26". This is the same angle of the line drawn in *The Book of the Law*.

This leads us to the mystery as to why Sirius is called the Dog Star. All dogs derive from the wolf, a much more popular and sacred animal when it comes to popular New Age thought. But, a dog is domesticated and obviously tamed to some degree. But, he is still a beast. The sexual rites of the Sirians might have included animals but more importantly, they accessed the beastly nature of man. This is why the dog was chosen. In a purely physical pleasure sense, the dog or man's beastly nature is man's best friend because it makes him feel good.

The Egyptians identified Set as *An* which means "the dog". This later begat the word "Set-an" and evolved into Satan who ruled hell, the infernal place of heat. The idea of a dog in heat is very much implied. This is where the morality play became "if you engage in bestiality, you'll go to hell". Actually, by definition, you were already in hell and it didn't feel that bad!

Perhaps the most intriguing mystery of all about the Dog Star is that "dog" is "god" spelled backwards. Both add up numerologically to the magic number 26, only this time the letters are in English and not Hebrew. What are the odds of this being a mere coincidence? All of this prompted Crowley to ask in *The Book of the Law* "Is a God to live in a dog?"

All of the above information will be somewhat indigestible to at least a few people's belief systems. For those who are very Christian oriented, it will help to remember Jesus's words: "Be as shrewd as the serpent but as gentle as the dove." It behooves us all to know all possible viewpoints. In fact, the Jesuit order drills their priests on how to be devil's advocates for heretical viewpoints.

In the above numerological correspondences between God and beast, we had to transpose the letters to get an equation of the two different words. If we look at the derivation of the word "God", we don't have to do any transposing and we get something of even more interest.

The English word "God" derives from the German *gott* which means to call or invoke. The word "invoke" derives from the Latin *vocare* which means to call and that in turn derives from the Old Norse word *kalla*. Only hypothetical derivations are offered for the word *kalla* by *Webster's New World Dictionary*. What the dictionary people don't know is that Old Norse was spoken by the Aryan race, the same people who "invaded" the subcontinent of India and gave us the Vedas and Hindu religion. This is a common historical fact. This religious lore was also accompanied by all the different systems of yoga including the sexual form of yoga known as tantra. The Aryans who gave the tantric arts to the Dravidian culture of India used the word *kala*.

Kala is a Sanskrit word meaning a vaginal vibration or a period of measured time. It also meant emanation of a divine essence and was represented by a flower, star, perfume or ray. Kala is also the source of Kali, the ancient Hindu goddess of time and the emanator of realities. Kalas are also represented by the different paths on the Cabalistic Tree of Life. By tapping into the kalas, one can reach the archetypes of existence and thereby shift consciousness. Kalas also correspond to the eight different colors (including black) and is the root of the word "color".

The most important kala was black and was called Kali. Black represents the void of creation from which all things are derived. It is another way of representing the mother principle. As the dark yuga rolled along, this type of magick or worship was lost in the ignorance of the times. It degenerated and was called black magic although it was not originally practiced in a negative or hurtful way. Black was a sacred color and was meant to represent the entire electromagnetic spectrum.

As periodic units of time measurement, kala is also the root of the word "calendar". It was in this sense that the manifestation of all the kalas, the goddess Kali, was considered most frightening for she had the power and ultimate responsibility to devour all of life. This is just one more manifestation of the Grim Reaper function in life. Time devours all living organisms.

The above derivation of the word "God" could obviously evolve into a whole theological dissertation in itself, but it should be apparent that the way the ancients worshiped creation was in complete reverse polarity compared to the common dogmas and belief systems of today.

Set or Shaitan is the oldest god in recorded history and it is quite possible that these Sumerians were the same Aryan race who settled in India. Set was also known as Sothis, Saturn and Sept, which is what September is named after. As the dark ages of the yuga occurred, the entire format of the religion of Set and the ancient rites were put into disrepute. Christians would later "satanize" Shaitan and incorporate this concept into an adversarial role in their religion. It was a derivation of this Sumerian religion that was carried forward into the time of the Knights Templars. The Church inquisitors would torture Templars "in the name of Christ" and tell them to renounce Satan. These Templars were not exactly the "evil" the church painted them to be; they merely had a different belief system.

The common denominators of the ancient Sumerian and Aryan religions (I suspect they both derived from the same source) seemed to revolve around the sexual process in the form of the Mother Goddess and the concept of time. Both were intimately related to consciousness itself. We have, of course, long since determined that sexual methods and time were essential to the Montauk operation. All of this information sets up a cross current of consciousness across the morphogenetic grid, most of which has been misunderstood and obscured in times past. Bringing it to light can change the consciousness for the future and teach us to learn from the mistakes of the past.

29

BABALON

According to tradition, the Sirians who originally settled in Sumeria had cat or lion like bodies. How many hybrids and just plain humans were absorbed into the ancient culture is not exactly known. What is known is that at some time they settled into the area of Cairo and called it Babalon or Babylon which meant Baby Lyon. This city was designated as one of the Sacred Places of the Lion and it was decided that a large repository of knowledge should be constructed nearby so as to preserve their collective wisdom. This construction project turned out to be what we know today as the Great Pyramid and the Sphinx. The Great Pyramid and its satellite pyramids were designed to serve as ancient time clocks that were in synchronization with the entire cyclic nature of the universe. The Sphinx represented the goddess in the form of Bast who was also known as Babalon and eventually Isis. To reiterate what was said earlier, the names Isis and Osiris were derived from Sirius.

In the Sphinx and Great Pyramid, the Sirians illustrated the two key principles of their religion. The two aspects were connected by sacred knowledge which could be found in the Hall of Records.

Aleister Crowley was schooled in all of this information. When he slept in the Great Pyramid prior to receiving *The Book of the Law*, he was seeking initiation with no strings attached. Projecting himself beyond his own understanding, he had a

profound experience. He connected with forms of consciousness that were not only far beyond the norm, they knew the
precise mathematics of the universe and this never ceased to
amaze him. The resultant effect was that he spent the rest of
his life trying to explain what had happened.

Earlier, we spoke of Tetragrammaton, the magical or alchemical formula that accompanied the "first tetrahedron" of
existence. The first element in alchemy or the tarot is fire and
is assigned to the first point of the tetrahedron of
Tetragrammaton. As fire itself forms a wave, the actual pattern
of that wave is reproduced to illustrate the vortex shape that
resides in the tetrahedron of Stan Tenon's work (as discussed
in Chapter 10). This is identical to the ram's horn and is also
the basis of the Hebrew fire letters whereby all the letters of
the alphabet could be perceived by rotating the shape within
the tetrahedron. With this much symbolism encoded in one
particular shape, it is easy to grasp that an energy stream of
consciousness is emitted from within the geometric matrix that
contains a tetrahedron or a pyramid. It is actually a conical
spiral of energy which conforms to a precise mathematical formula known as the Fibonacci spiral. That this cone of energy
can influx a mind with extra intelligence was illustrated in history by placing a dunce cap on a slow student. The cone on the
head was supposed to make him smarter but evolved into a
punishment style degradation of the student concerned. Although Crowley was not known to wear a dunce cap, he did
use a magician's hat for some occasions which is really the
same thing.

The fire or primal energy of Tetragrammaton that exists
in the Great Pyramid was linked to the fire and passion of the
Sphinx through the passageway known as the Hall of Records.
The Sphinx represents the lustful and unrestricted loins of Bast
but also the intelligent female Virgo (known to the Romans as
Diana, Goddess of the Moon) who transmutes the lower energies into the higher form. In other words, she could tap into the
Hall of Records. When Crowley performed sexual magick, he
was often trying to tap into the higher consciousness portrayed

in the Hall of Records. He was using the lower energies to tap the higher.

The Great Pyramid itself is a very curious structure for many different reasons. One of its more intriguing features is that it is not a symmetrical polygon. In other words, if you consider the Great Pyramid to be the upper half of an octahedron, you would expect two angles at the base of each triangular surface to measure 60° each. This is not the case. The angles at the base of each triangle are 51.51°. This means that the pyramid has been squashed. In other words, you would get the same result if you took a perfectly symmetrical octahedron and pushed the top and bottom towards the center. The angles would shift under the force exerted. The reason for this is that the Earth itself is not a perfect sphere. It is a spheroid, i.e. it looks like a tangerine. What this is telling us is that the matrix lines which make up the blueprint for the Earth are not perfectly symmetrical either. They may have been in their original condition, but whenever the Earth was squashed into a spheroid or otherwise assumed that particular shape, the corresponding grid lines assumed the shape of the Earth and were distorted accordingly. The 51.51° angles of the Great Pyramid correspond exactly to the geometric distortion of the Earth from a sphere to its current shape. What this means is that whoever built the Great Pyramid knew the exact shape of the Earth's grid.

There is another interesting aspect when you consider the angles of the Great Pyramid. When it was in its heyday, the pyramid was encased in limestone which is really just calcium carbonate. If you put this chemical under a microscope and apply a protractor to what you see, you will discover that calcium carbonate also consists of two 51.51° angles at the base of each triangular molecule. In other words, the molecules in the limestone facing of the pyramid were mimicking the very shape of the Great Pyramid which mimics the Earth's grid itself. Taking this a step further, calcium carbonate is what human bones are made of. This is why the dead bones of the Montauks were so important to tapping into the grid. The geometry of the bones was in complete resonance to the pyramidal structure of the grid. Of course, all human bones have this property. They resonate energy which can include consciousness as well. And if you don't believe that bones can influence consciousness, try scaring the living daylights out of somebody through the use of a skeleton. Actually, you shouldn't. It works only too well.

In his different works, Crowley hints that he knew these various aspects of the Great Pyramid and its energies. Using this, along with his other knowledge which included an extensive study of the Sumerians, he created specific rituals that were designed not only to reach other planes of consciousness but to communicate with unseen worlds by every conceivable means. This was very much intended to include aliens.

In 1918, Crowley began a sexual magick operation with a lady in New York by the name of Roddie Minor. It was known as the Amalantrah Working and was done just a few months before he spent the summer at Montauk Point. One of the main features in this working was the symbolism of the egg. They were told, "it's all in the egg". This corresponds exactly to the sacred geometry precepts given earlier in this book. The egg is the first sphere of existence and all the potential that unfolds thereafter. The entity contacted was LAM and an artistic rendering of him by Crowley looks hauntingly familiar to the gray aliens we have all heard so much about. LAM's bulbous head has the shape of an egg.

Documents of the OTO indicate that LAM is the Tibetan word for Way or Path and that a LAMA is "He who Goeth". The Tibetan connection appearing in Crowley's work just before he traveled to Montauk is interesting and should be noted. Earlier, we defined the Tibetan word "mantak" as clarity or understanding. In the Amalantrah Working, Crowley was told "Thou art to go this Way". It is easy to associate LAM with Montauk although the connection warrants further research. But it is certain that Montauk does connect to Tibet, not only through the word "mantak" but by virtue of the German connection mentioned earlier in this book.

Of additional interest concerning LAM is that it is a Celtic word for door jam and implies a stop on the path as opposed to a pathway. There is also an ancient land in present day Iraq that was known as Elam. It is located on the northeast banks of the Tigris River at the beginning of the Persian Gulf. The language spoken in Elam was a curiosity as it had no known relationship with any other language.

There is also current interest in LAM today. The OTO has founded a Cult of Lam for their members who are drawn to this entity and want to use the egg as an astral space-capsule for travelling to Lam's domain and for tantric time travelling.

The main point concerning LAM is that Crowley was contacting an extraterrestrial entity who had links to almost every aspect we've studied. The idea that Crowley continued to function in some aspect of LAM after his death in 1947 is a possibility especially when you consider that is the year when the rash of UFO sightings began.

The year 1947 has an amazing correspondence in itself and that has to do with a major grid point that has been found to exist on different planets. It was discovered that Cydonia, the region of Mars that houses the face and the pyramids, rests at 19.47° from the equator. The same can be said for the whirling red spot on Jupiter and a similar area found on Neptune. On our planet Earth, pyramids are exactly at 19.47° north of the equator on the Yucatan peninsula in Mexico. I have also been informed by someone who just recently visited the island of Hawaii that pyramids have been found there but are covered with jungle vegetation. They are at 19.47° north of the equator as well.

None of this proves that Aleister Crowley or his death in 1947 is responsible for the UFO sightings since that time period, but many people have noticed and commented upon it along with the UFO crash at Roswell, New Mexico that occurred in the same year. Actually, Crowley's death occurred on December 1st which was well after the Roswell incident. Of course, we could argue that he was weak and dying and that was why the military in New Mexico were able to shoot down "his" flying saucers with their SAGE Radar. That is an unlikely scenario, but whatever the case is with Crowley, it is undeniable that he deeply influenced another magician who has been inextricably linked to aliens, the CIA and Montauk. That man is Jack Parsons and his grand experiment was in 1946.

Jack Parsons was described in *Montauk Revisited* as having conducted a sexual magick experiment that has been hailed by some as the magical experiment of the century. This activity was done in conjunction with two magicians who were part of the Wilson Clan: Marjorie Cameron and L. Ron Hubbard. The experiment was called the Babalon Working and was designed to invoke the Mother Goddess in her crowning glory: she who is called Babalon.

I have done a considerable amount of research into Jack Parsons since *Montauk Revisited* was published. He deserves an entire book and only a very brief summary of what I've found can be included here.

Jack was a cofounder of the Jet Propulsion Laboratory and his innovations in rocketry made our space program a reality. He died officially on June 17, 1952 as the result of a chemical explosion in his laboratory, but a search through all the newspapers and a talk with his wife and a friend revealed mysterious circumstances. His wife, Marjorie Cameron, arrived after the explosion but before the ambulance had left. The attendants would not let her ride in the ambulance nor was she allowed to see him in the hospital. What is most outrageous is that the police violated standard procedure when they omitted asking her to identify the body. She was Jack's next of kin as his mother was declared dead from suicide after hearing the report that Jack had died. Neither Cameron nor George Frey, who took care of Jack's cremation, saw the actual dead body. Further, the newspaper accounts are filled with suspicious characters and accounts. The death of Virginia Parsons, Jack's mother, had equally bizarre circumstances surrounding it.

I asked the Pasadena police department if I could look at the file for the case. They said it was old and that I should write to the microfiche department. If it wasn't sealed, I should be able to review it. I wrote them a letter requesting permission to review the relevant files and after a long delay, I was told that the file was purged from their system. I do know that the FBI watched his every move. Maybe somebody will provide that file someday.

While the circumstances surrounding Jack's death are a mystery, his magical career is not so murky. He was perhaps more passionate and dedicated to the Mother Goddess than any popular magician of the century. Crowley and Jack did not see eye to eye about the Babalon Working. Crowley was at the end of his life and Jack was playing the part of the wayward and rebellious son. According to reports, Crowley wrote him off as a failure, but he did leave a door open. He said that he hadn't received an expected report from Parsons and that a final conclusion would have to remain open.

When Jack conducted the Babalon Working in 1946, he invoked the goddess Babalon and sought to bring an end to the tyranny which had dominated mankind during the dark yuga. That he at least had an idea of what he was doing can be seen by virtue of the yantra he used. A yantra is a two dimensional glyph that is designed to evoke a fourth dimensional experience. It is a common device in magick, yoga and other meditative arts. The yantra that was used for the Babalon Working was the seven pointed star and has been reproduced on the following page. Note that the seven letters of Babalon fit into the triangles. In this glyph, all the angles are designed to be 51.51°. These are the same angles of the Great Pyramid of Giza which found their numerical value as a result of the pyramid being structured so as to be in harmony with the Earth's grid. If you multiply 51.51 by seven, you get 360.57, the approximate length of an ancient calendar year. It was by this means that the Babalon workers (Jack, Ron and Cameron) were plugging into the consciousness of the time line. What happened to the participants after they entered their altered states of consciousness is still anyone's guess. But, they did project themselves out of this reality and the consequent result and

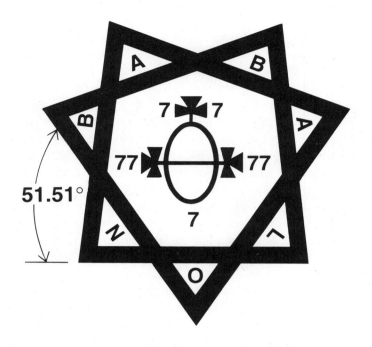

THE BABALON YANTRA

A yantra is a geometrical representation of a mantra (sound waves) that correspond to a particular deity, in this case Babalon. The yantra and mantra are both meaningless unless activated by magical application to the consciousness of the practitioner which is called tantra. The illustration on the opposite page is an artistic rendition of "The Star" card from the Tarot. The star in the picture is identical to the above yantra and is identified as the seven pointed star of Venus or Babalon whose primary characteristic is love. Behind all existence lies the principle of the mother goddess. Common people refer to this phenomena as Mother Nature. Magicians call it Babalon and invoke her in an attempt to create further strands of evolution. [NOTE: The above illustration is a literal duplication of an actual drawing from Jack Parsons' workbook. If the yantra is drawn correctly the angle demarcated in the drawing will be exactly 51.51°. The drawing as given is off by a few degrees.]

XVII

The Star

synchronicity of the act has led in no small part to the writing of this book.

Cameron has said that the operation changed Jack and Ron Hubbard forever. They were never quite the same. After recovering from a paralysis on his right side (as a result of the working), Hubbard eventually accessed incredible genius and a considerable amount of energy. Most of this was channeled into the Dianetics and Scientology movement. He had people doing regressions on alien implants forty years before it became vogue.

Parsons took a different route. Always considered a security risk by the military industrial complex, he continued his pursuit of magick. He had completed the Babalon Working ritual itself, but the consequent chain reactions and results still had to reach their appointed conclusions.

Concerning the Babalon Working, Jack wrote a statement to the effect that he would be consumed by the fire. Whether he meant this in an allegorical or real sense, we don't know. It was said in honor of Babalon and he was willing to serve as the supreme sacrifice. Just a few months before his reported death, he foresaw that some kind of end was near. He knew that this end could mean physical death and he didn't rule it out.

There is yet a greater mystery that has been overlooked by many. Although Jack was on the outs with the OTO after the Babalon Working, he had obtained the Ninth Degree in the order. In order to progress beyond that grade, one has to give up their identity. There is no question that this was accomplished. Whether he assumed a secret identity within the confines of the secret government or simply died is not known. That he might have died physically is rather insignificant in the higher scheme of things. But, he did change his identity. Jack Parsons has been legally dead for forty years.

Another fact about Jack that is often overlooked or not mentioned is that he was not only a member of the OTO but was a member of the A∴A∴. No mention is ever made of him having ever fallen out of grace with that particular order which is, of course, the Illuminati. What is of further interest in this regard is that Cameron once told me that she gave Jack's birth time to some of the top astrologers in Southern California. They told her his chart indicated he was or could be the real head of the CIA.

As Crowley and Parsons were both members of the Illuminati, we have to take a look at what the organization is and what it actually represents. From what has been said already, we know that it is related to Sirius. There are also countless books and conspiracy theories on the subject. According to the dictionary, the Illuminati refers to those of a secret society who profess to have special intellectual or spiritual enlightenment.

Let us next consider what happens when someone achieves a brilliant illumination and transcends all experience known. He goes into another dimension and basically understands the entire picture of creation. This is sometimes referred to as a kundalini experience or tapping into the universal consciousness. There are, of course, many types and variations of illuminations. I am referring to a particularly grand one. When one achieves such a state, he is still left with the predicament of relating to the Earth plane which has its share of imperfection and turmoil. If one person achieves such a state, it does not automatically transfer to the entire human race.

All of this catapults us right into the war of consciousness. There are those of us who want to be more aware and expand the consciousness across the entire parameters of existence. There are also those who want to limit such activity. Splendorous and gigantic scenarios can be recognized or imagined that pit various secret groups against one another.

Most important to our investigation, Aleister Crowley and Jack Parsons were plugged into a tradition that identified with the Illuminati and sought to expand consciousness. Whether their activities were good or bad is not the point. Both of their writings reflect the fact that they were warriors for consciousness. Those who decried them seemed to be on the other side of the coin.

Aleister Crowley's goal was to set occult forces in motion that would result in the illumination of all by the end of this century. Jack Parsons followed in the same tradition but the circumstances of his death at a young age leave a different enigma. We are forced to consider whether he lived and has orchestrated forces in a super secret capacity or whether he died and did the same thing from the spirit world. The bottom line is that his magick has reverberated and created effects beyond his own ordinary mortal means. Both men encountered dark forces in their work and neither were afraid to deal with them. They have also chosen dark vehicles by which to communicate. But, ultimately, what did they communicate? That all creation manifests from the light, also defined as the electromagnetic spectrum which is just another word for Mother Nature.

Crowley offered us all a clue when he announced he wouldn't officially assume the name "Phoenix" until the work was completed. In this regard, the true Phoenix Project would be to redeem mankind by purging the forces of ignorance and oppression that have ruled during the last 13,000 years.

Armageddon awaits us all, but not in the sense it has been perpetrated on us by the merchants of fear and those with ulterior motives. For each of us, it will be a personal encounter, if it hasn't been encountered already. In one corner will be the Christ with all the angelic forces he can muster. In the other, will be the Antichrist with his demons. Those of us who invoke the wisdom of Babalon will not be rooting in the corner of either side. We'll be functioning as the referee and ensuring that each side fights fair with no bribes being offered to the World Boxing Council by some of those notorious mystery school people who sit in the expensive front row seats. If we can accomplish that, the fight should go the distance and be declared a draw. Ascension will occur.

On the Day of Judgement, there shall be no judgement. At least, if there is, those who are doing the judging won't be following Christ's words: "Judge not, lest ye be judged".

So, as they say at Caesar's Palace: "Let's get ready to rumble!"

30

REQUIEM

As we leave the projections of consciousness that have brought us to the very heights of the Illuminati looking through the Eye of Horus, we must return to Earth and the point from which we departed: Montauk Point. This is where the desecration of the Native American tradition reached its all time high in terms of turning one's back on ancient knowledge and the supporting pagan belief system which honored it.

As was said towards the beginning of this book, the name Parsons has figured synchronously regarding the Montauk tribe. It was a Colonel William Parsons who indentured Stephen Talkhouse Pharoah as a young man. The Montauks' property was first auctioned off in the home of the Parsons family. When the mounds and various geometric relics of the Mound Builders were discovered in Ohio in the late 1700s, it was a Samuel Holden Parsons who showed a sudden interest in the mounds and was sent on behalf of the U.S. Government to acquire the land from the local Native Americans. Parsons was a friend of George Washington (a Freemason who also commissioned the Montauk Lighthouse) and may have done his land acquisition as the result of a presidential order. This is unclear at this point, but Washington did appoint him as judge of the Northwest Territory. Thomas Jefferson also got personally involved with the mound relics. Samuel Parsons died in a mysterious drowning accident at Big Beaver River, Ohio, on November 17, 1789.

213

Many years after his death, an investigation was done which revealed he had acted in concert with the British so as to betray the revolution.

What is remarkable in all these instances is that the name Parsons seems to have had oppressive influence over the Native American culture. There is no reason to believe that Jack Parsons himself was in opposition to the Native American tradition at all, but after his death in 1952, a new television program made its way onto the air waves which was dedicated to denigrating the Native American culture. It was called *The Lone Ranger* and was popular with children through the early 1960s. The Lone Ranger was a cowboy do-gooder who went around stopping bad guys in their tracks. He was always assisted by Tonto, his faithful Indian companion who often served as an interpreter but was never shown to have much prestige. Tonto was a "good Indian" who seemed to see the infinite wisdom of the white man's ways. What is particularly remarkable about this show is that Tonto always referred to the Lone Ranger as "Kee-ma-sabee". This is actually a phonetic spelling for the Spanish words *Que el mas sabe* which means "he who knows more". In Spanish, the word "tonto" means stupid.

The Lone Ranger also made a point of always using silver bullets. Perhaps he thought his enemies were shape shifting werewolves or maybe these silver bullets were a symbolic death wish to the Manitou, the shape shifting gods of the Native Americans. One has to wonder how much subtlety was deliberately orchestrated by the writers. It was certainly rubbing salt in the wounds of the Native American culture which includes the tradition of the Manitou.

The Manitou were the sacred shamans of all Native Americans and were masters of time travel and shape shifting. Known as the Great Spirits, they believed that all creatures should evolve according to their own nature and that all wisdom or enlightenment was earned. Incarnate upon the Earth hundreds of years of ago, they decided to depart as they foresaw the denigration of their natural ways and of the Native American beliefs.

The prophecies and departure of the Manitou came to the forefront in 1869 when a Paiute mystic by the name of Wodzuwob or Tavibo prophesied the doom of the whites and that the return of all Native American ancestors would come as the result of a dance ceremony. His son, Wowoka, took everything a step further when he had his own vision of dying twice and being resurrected. Seeing God, he was told that a flood of water and mud would cover the Earth and destroy white civilization. But, if his people did the round dance, the flood would roll under them. All Native Americans would then return to the Earth and enjoy an eternal existence free from suffering.

Wowoka began preaching his vision in 1886 but said that Native Americans had to earn their way to this new world. He opposed violence against whites but composed songs for the traditional round dance which became known as the Ghost Dance. All of this turned into the Ghost Dance religion which spread throughout the entire west. Some of the Native Americans did not embrace the non violent philosophy of Wowoka. The Sioux Nation did their version of the Ghost Dance which was perceived as hostile by the whites. When the Ghost Dance was banned and the Sioux continued, hostilities broke out which resulted in the death of Sitting Bull. After that, on December 29, 1890, a band of Native Americans were ordered to camp at Wounded Knee Creek. When a shot broke out, a massacre ensued and that was virtually the end of serious opposition to white civilization.

I don't know if Wowoka's vision will come true. That depends upon what sort of information is pumped into the morphogenetic grid. We should all learn a lesson from Wowoka though. His anglicized name was Jack Wilson! At this stage in the Montauk investigation, it should surprise no one that the name Wilson would appear, let alone the first name of Jack. But this was not the only synchronicity that would rhyme with the legacy of Montauk.

Another remarkable coincidence would occur upon meeting with the Montauk Shaman for the second time. We met at

215

Lion Gardiner Park in the town of Bayshore. The name Lion Gardiner is ironic because he was the first one to "swindle" the Montauks out of their land. The first name "Lion" has other implications which you already understand by now. The Shaman wanted to do some sort of ceremonial initiation with me, but I had no idea of what she had in mind. Just before I left my house, I received a phone call from Denney Colt who said she would like to come along. The three of us walked a nature path to a bay which overlooks the island upon which Duncan Cameron lives. That seemed rather odd for starters.

The Shaman had Denney draw a circle in the sand. Then she asked me what it meant. I said it represented Alpha and Omega, the first and last words of the Greek alphabet which represent the beginning and the end. Together, they symbolize the circle of infinity. I guess I passed that test. The Shaman then drew a cross in the middle of the circle which was the exact glyph shown in *The Book of the Law*: a cross within a circle. She asked me what this meant. I had just discovered the meaning of this glyph a few days earlier and the timing was astounding. I answered her with a full paragraph. The Shaman understood although she has not studied Aleister Crowley. She appreciated what I was saying because this symbol was known by all the ancient mystics. It was simply passed on down through her own shamanic heritage. The synchronicity in this instance was amazing but was topped when Denney told us that she had just finished making a piece of jewelry with the exact same symbol.

This experience reiterates the importance of the circle and the cross and how its imprint on the mind can tap into the morphogenetic grid. It is one of the oldest symbols in the universe. When the cross and circle are put into three dimensions, it becomes the basis for energy and the evolution of all existence. It is also the basis for what occurred at Montauk during the Montauk Project. Those operators knew how to entrain the human condition or how to regress it. They knew how to tap into the morphogenetic grid. These operators were the mystery schools and there was no shortage of them or their under-

216

lings feeding different information into the grid. After a time, the entire scenario became very unbalanced.

As the various mystery schools operated through Montauk, they were putting a negative spin in evolution when they could have been using their knowledge to imprint higher circuitry in the brain and allowing people to wake up. This still needs to be done but the Montauk grid is still being bombarded by various electronic transmissions of a strictly artificial nature. In this respect, it is like a diseased energy right now that has to be healed.

The only ones that really have permission to accomplish that healing are the owners of the land or the keepers of the gate. By "owners" I am referring to the whole aspect of the lineage that owns the land and is responsible for maintaining the consciousness thereof. Whether they are shaken from their property and whether or not the deed says so, the Montauks are still the true owners.

Just before this book went to the printer, I had the honor of being invited to the Montauks annual Thanksgiving celebration sponsored by the Miller Ridge Inn in Jericho, Long Island. I was surprised to see that the New York city television stations were covering it as a Native American event. When I was invited to get up and say a few words, the media couldn't have packed out the door any faster. It was like a programmed response and one of the Montauks told me it was intentional and very rude.

I spoke briefly to the Montauks, just touching on the Montauk Project which most of them hadn't heard of. My focus was on the family name of Pharoah, the pyramids, Montauk's role as a sacred site and the restoration of their rights to the land. I was again surprised when I was approached by one of the medicine women who thanked me for talking of the pyramids. She said that her grandfather had told her about the pyramids but no one ever believed her. They were composed of rocks from the end of Montauk Point and were located at Camp Hero or not far away. Her grandfather had said that past generations had done underground ceremonies beneath the pyramids. They were eventually covered by sand and were not necessarily the white brick like pyramids mentioned earlier.

The Montauk tribe has now been generally informed regarding the general nature of why their property was seized accompanied by the desecration of their ancient heritage. Some of them also know more than they say which is their prerogative as Native Americans. They will speak when they are ready. Ultimately, the Montauks are the ones that must heal the grid. It is the bones of their ancestors which contain the encrypted secrets of the past in resonance with the geometric patterns of the morphogenetic grid. The energies have to be cleansed and purified and then the secrets can be relinquished.

Regardless of deeds and who holds temporary possession of the land, the true owners of the land will always be resonating with the consciousness of the people and the morphogenetic grid. Although it is really just surfacing with this book, there has been an underlying power working to make the Montauks clearly see the extent of their responsibility. By implementing the ancestral consciousness of the Pharoah family, they can permeate the consciousness of the grid and clean it up.

The first step in this process has been for the Shaman of the Montauks to declare an amnesty to all beings who have participated in the desecration of the Montauk Holy Land. This includes all crimes against humanity and against the morphogenetic process of evolution itself. It would also apply to those bureaucrats, officials or other individuals who have in any way sought to hamper the investigation of the truth concerning the secretive phenomena that has occurred at Camp Hero or the general vicinity of Montauk.

To accept this amnesty (if it applies to you), it is only required that you recognize what you have done. Any atonements are between you and your creator and should be sorted out accordingly. If your information is noteworthy for investigative purposes, see that it gets into the proper hands and is not withheld from those who need to know. Those who would like to confess their crimes for spiritual purposes, may write their transgressions to the Shaman. She may be addressed care of the publisher or by writing to Montauk Shaman, PO Box 454, Bayshore, New York, 11706.

This amnesty is being extended on behalf of the Montauk Shaman and her own spiritual authority. It is not being done on my behalf as I have such authority. I would only ask that all of you in the reading audience do whatever is in your power, whether it be large or small, to assist the Montauks in getting their land back. Their task and responsibilities are not small and they need all the help they can get.

It would be inappropriate to say anything else at this point. Thank you for listening and being aware.

NOTE: Since the writing of the first edition, the blood descendant and royal heir of the Montauks, Robert Pharoah, has come forth to claim his heritage as Grand Sachem of the Montauks. This came as a surprise as I had previously spoken to his mother Olive but didn't even know that he existed. There are reportedly forty royal blood descendants immediately connected to the Pharoah family who have previously had severe differences of opinion with those members of the Montauk tribe I had consulted.

Although the Pharoahs had not previously given formal recognition to either Bob Cooper as Tribal Leader or Sharon Jackson as Shaman, we are happy to report that all have united in a tribal council in an attempt to reconcile all differences of opinion and form a united front by which the Montauks can retrieve their rightful properties.

This addition was written at the request of Olive Pharoah who would like everyone to know there is yet another side to this unfolding story. Further updates on the Montauks efforts to regain their land will be covered in The Montauk Pulse newsletter which is described in the back of this book.

219

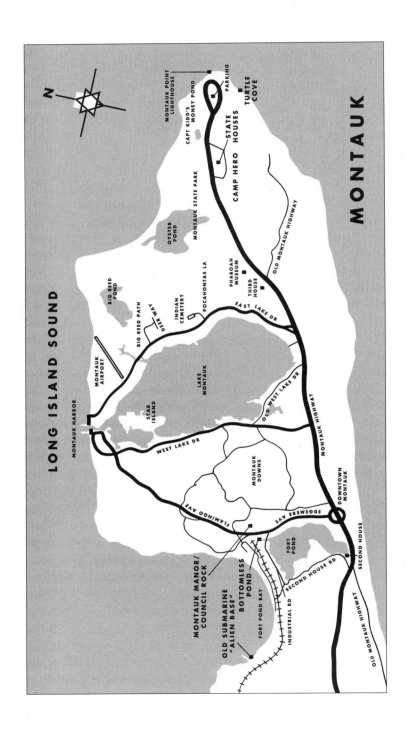

PART
II

BY PRESTON B. NICHOLS

INTRODUCTION
TO PART II

I would like to start off by being the first one to accept the amnesty that the Montauk Shaman has so kindly extended to all those who have participated in the desecration of the sacred Native American grounds. My participation in the Montauk Project is now well known although some aspects of my involvement remain hidden even to myself.

Further, I would like to accept the amnesty for a transgression I made at Council Rock. While visiting the site with Peter, Duncan and a couple of other friends, I made a verbal slight by saying it was just a rock. As I returned to my van, I said to myself that there was nothing special about the rock. I tripped on a stone at that very moment and twisted my foot quite badly. The result was a week of severe pain, and I believe this was a lesson for me. Council Rock is sacred and belongs to the Natives, as does the rest of the land they are requesting be returned to them.

I will now embark upon a general update of other events that have occurred since the writing of *Montauk Revisited* in 1993. We will begin with a general history of the Montauk underground and follow its development up to 1994. After that will be an update on the Montauk Boys, an account of irregular transmissions at the base and a technical description of the particle accelerator that Peter mentioned at the beginning of this book. Finally, I will end on a short description of the time line which will complement that information in Part I.

I should also mention that I am frequently besieged by people who want more technical information about Montauk. The general description given in *The Montauk Project* is just

223

that: a general description. The little bit of technical information offered in this book and *Montauk Revisited* is offered because it is directly related to the unveiling of the mysteries of Montauk. It is not really economically practical to publish dissertations on detailed technical aspects of Montauk without doing it in a cohesive manner. This would mean a very large and expensive volume that would be directed at a very narrow audience.

It is also very well known to me that many technical people are interested in anything I have to say whether they think my stories are off the wall or not. Some are even angry that I don't tell more. Essentially, they want me to do their research. I am also highly skeptical of why they would want to build a time machine. These same people are usually not very spiritually evolved and might recreate a disaster like Montauk if they were to harness certain technology.

These are two of the basic reasons I can't tell you more about the technical aspects of time travel. The other reason is that I honestly don't know everything. I was a cog in a big machine at Montauk and was used as much as anyone else. As the mysteries of Montauk and elsewhere unfold, we will arrive at an understanding of where we are supposed to be, all in its due course.

31

THE MONTAUK
UNDERGROUND

The Montauk underground fascinates many people to the point where they go out to Montauk and look for it. This is not a good idea for two reasons. One, the entrances are concealed and the people who are aware of them are not likely to let you penetrate them. Two, if you find an entrance or tunnel you immediately encounter a new set of problems. If you are "lucky" enough to find an entrance, it will take a minor military reconaissance operation just to investigate what you find. The tunnels are miles in length and the distances to cover are vast, if they are not sealed or otherwise blocked. One would need abundant lighting, food and a lot of time. Tunneling gear would also be a likely requisite. Then, if you find a hot installation, who knows what might happen. You could expect very unfriendly faces. Please keep all of this in mind when you visit Montauk and don't act foolishly.

The underground at Montauk is not really a secret but information about it has been deliberately obscured. People do find references to it now and then. If you consult a geodesic survey or contour map from before 1940, you will notice that there is a rising hill coming out of the town of Montauk. Then, the road is flat from that point out to the lighthouse. If you look at a map from the 1960s, you'll find that there are more hills after the first one that extend out to the end of the point. I believe those hills are man made. The explanation for all this centers around the fact that Camp Hero was an army base from the 1940s up to around the late 1960s. You actually had to go through a military check point to get to the lighthouse which is on Government property to this day. The purchase of the lighthouse was made by Alexander Hamilton on orders from President Washington.

In about 1940, there was a major construction project. A huge group of buildings were constructed in two levels. Below this, two levels of cellars were built. After these were finished, they were covered with dirt and became the two hills you will see at the base today. This is how Radar Hill (which is where the transmitter tower sits) came about.

The bunkers were refurbished from older ones which were built in the 1920s. This date is ascertained upon inspection of the antiquated wiring that was left behind. The bunkers were rebuilt to blend in with the new underground facilities. After all the construction was done, there was a four level underground which could serve as a very large air raid shelter for use by the Government. It was set up so that all Federal officials in the entire northeast could harbor there in case of an attack on that part of the country. Although Camp Hero's role in history has been deliberately obscured, it is a fact that it was once the headquarters of the Air Force's Defense efforts in the northeast.

By the time the Montauk Project got underway in the late 1960s, there was a six level underground facility in use. Two levels were added in about 1950. This was learned through reports that a project was launched to shore up Montauk Point so that the lighthouse would not fall into the ocean. Excavation of hard rocks from the underground were broken into bits, covered with sand, and placed around the point. Substantiating this is an individual I know who lived out there in the 1960s and witnessed a curiousity while walking around by the cliffs. He saw a big hole at the end of a cliff and saw a big bucket loader emerge from the hole and drop some dirt over the end of the cliff. This was probably an extension to the 6th level of underground. The rocks used to shore up the point may have been transported through this hole or one like it.

I have also received reports from witnesses who say there are now eight levels of underground at Montauk. This corresponds with other reports that huge boulders started appearing at the point in the late '80s and early '90s. The boulders are roughly 10 feet wide by 6 feet high and are about 12 or 15 feet long. They are reportedly dynamited into smaller rocks as described earlier. These huge rocks suddenly showing up at the point forces us to ask some simple questions. First, how did the rocks get there? My friends and I have asked if anyone ever saw a flat bed bringing them out. The answer was no; besides, it would have taken an awful lot of trucks which would have been very noticeable coming through town. Second, did they use a barge? For a barge to leave rocks at the point, it would have had to have gotten close to shore and would require a deep draught of water. The point is not deep enough for a barge of any depth to approach the point.

At a Montauk lecture on Long Island one night, someone said they once saw a trap door open up at the end of the point. A huge rock came sliding out of the opening and then the door would close. This explanation along with the other reports mentioned offer a good explanation for the source of the boulders because Montauk is essentially a mountain that comes up from the ocean floor. At about level six or seven of the underground, you are excavating rock. The rocks that have appeared in recent times and can still be seen at this writing could be debris from levels 7 and 8 of the underground.

The above is evidence that there is an underground. I will now describe its size and general nature as per various reports and some of my own memories.

Levels 1 and 2 are spotty. They consist of a group of buildings that are connected by tunnels. On the average, each building is about 1,000 by 500 feet. At certain locales, they might reach out to within 100 ft of the shore. Levels 3 and 4 extend about a mile to the north and south of Camp Hero. They are continuous and extend to the ocean. They extend about a half mile to the east and maybe two or three miles west. Levels 5 and 6 are about the same as Levels 3 and 4 except that they extend under the town of Montauk through to about the Fort Pond area. Level 7 is even more extensive and goes out five miles to the north, south, and east of Radar Hill. To the west, it goes about about 10 miles to the Napeague Strip. Level 8 is fairly small because it is still under construction. I've been told that levels 5, 6 and 7 are like an underground city.

There is another piece of strange business concerning the underground when we consider the Montauk Tower in the center of town, just north of the traffic circle. It is a likely location to house underground workers because there are never any cars parked there, yet people I know have tried to rent there and have been told it is fully occupied. If you happen to see as many as six cars in the parking lot, it is highly unusual. It was also reported by one lady who looked at the rooms that they were surprisingly small. This opens the door to the possibility that it may have been designed for aliens. All in all, this building is just one more enigma in the town of Montauk.

There is yet more information to suggest a Montauk underground. When the Montauk Project went haywire in 1983, the underground was more or less shut down until about 1987. Evidence has surfaced that there were contracts issued in 1987 for maintenance of underground levels associated with the Montauk Air Force station. This indicates that things were reactivated at about that time period. It probably took about four years to completely refurbish. It should be noted that it was never a plush place.

One of the biggest smoking guns pointing to an active underground exists on a green maintenance garage within the grounds of Camp Hero. It is manned and houses a large industrial watt hour meter that is up in the megawatt range. Why do they need megawatts of power going into the maintenance garage? If they dissipated that amount of power in the garage, it would burn the place down. It has to be going to the underground.

Considerable power is still being carried into the state

park. At least 20 megawatts are going in at this writing and it might be as high as 60 or 70 megawatts. There are at least two separate lines. One comes in from the east to the garage. The other comes in from the west. According to LILCO (Long Island Lighting Company), these two lines have separate sources and do not join underground despite what some people out at Montauk say. The lines are very large and are not for any normal type of usage.

At the same time we have a bright new shiny power plant that has appeared out at Montauk. It is actually more than a few years old but it is an anomaly. The town says it is a backup source of power for the town of Montauk. If I go by my own normal estimates, it is about a 20 megawatt plant. That is enough to supply the whole South Fork of Long Island with power under emergency conditions. What does a sleepy little fishing village like Montauk need with that size power plant? LILCO engineers I know say it is actually a 100 megawatt plant. If so, it would have to be a power plant for a gigantic facility.

In addition to the backup station at Montauk, there is also another power facility in the town of East Hampton, just near the railroad tracks. From the air, this power facility is accompanied by a circular area just acroos the tracks. This indicates a particle accelerator (which you can read about in Chapter Thirty-five). My friend at LILCO will not comment on the facility in East Hampton. He says not to ask because he can't talk about it. I suspect it may be a gigawatt plant. That's enough power to run most of the northeastern United States.

In addition to the normal LILCO power lines, we have two big power generating facilities on the South Fork of Long Island. For what? They are probably used to run particle accelerators.

Another interesting point about the South Fork is that almost no one who owns property east of East Hampton has the mining rights to their property. This suggests the possibility that underground facilities could run all the way to East Hampton. I don't really know. The large power generator in East Hampton leaves me to wonder if the underground extends all the way to East Hampton. Further investigation may prove it.

Another lead to the underground surfaced when a Government contract was issued in around 1991 to do a toxic clean up of the Montauk Air Force Station. Nothing was done until about 1993 and plenty of work has been done since that point. Many buildings have been torn down with holes being dug all over the grounds. This takes on meaning if you consider my own theory about the Congressional investigation of Montauk. I have spoken to congressmen about Montauk who are interested and have told me they are conducting their own investigation. Unfortunately, they say it will take a long time because they have to go through all sorts of red tape. I was also told that Peter Moon and myself would probably be the last ones to find out the results of any such investigation.

The current Montauk Project may be doing everything they can to obscure any evidence of an underground. It is my theory that they are demolishing buildings and digging holes in order to dig out and seal up any entrances to the underground. The cement is removed and the area is filled in. This way, when Congress or other agencies come out to investigate, they will be misled. If investigators refer to the Army Corps of Engineers map, they will see an entrance. The Montauk crew will then show them that the area has been dug out and sealed off. Investigators will then assume that because there are no entrances, the underground is not in use.

There is probably an underground entrance in the town of Montauk itself as well as the green maintenance garage. In the case of the garage, it probably leads to a derelict underground which would be readily shown to investigators. But, if the investigators knew exactly where to go in this region, they would probably find an active underground.

This whole line of reasoning began when my ability to access the base was short circuited. I agreed with Judge Ketcham not to go onto the restricted area of the base. At this point, I began taking overhead flights of the area with a 2,000 speed shutter video camera. Even though the camera gets jerked around during the motion of the airplane, each frame is crystal clear and I can see what is going on. From this, I could see the holes being dug and the buildings being torn down.

There were also other anomolies. One was this smokestack they had left standing. It was left after a steam generating plant (that had supplied the heating plant) was torn down. One of my friends who works on demolition and construction told me that you always tear down a smokestack first. That way, it won't fall on you when you demolish the rest of the building. In fact, he said it is very dangerous to leave one standing. There had to be a reason that the smokestack was left on the base. It probably connects to the underground in some fashion.

The existence of the underground was given another vote of confidence when my video recordings revealed asbestos covered piping. Two of the main points in the contract to detoxify the base called for removal of asbestos and PCB (PCB refers to polychlorinated biphenoles, a type of transformer oil) transformers. They did seem to dig up the PCB transformers, but they left the asbestos sitting in the open. This is noticeable in my video footage of pipes with white covering running all around the base. The white covering was asbestos. These had been part of a piping system that distributed steam and hot water to heat all the buildings from a central plant.

According to EPA (Environmental Protection Agency) requirements, the workers cannot go within two hundred feet of these pipes without a special suit. As the buildings were being demolished, these asbestos pipes were just left on the ground. According to the detoxing contract, the first thing they should've removed is those pipes. Asbestos left out in the open air and wind is very dangerous. All of this tells us that the detox contract is not what it was purported to be. The evidence is on my tapes. The contract is a cover and probably ties into my theory about sealing the underground in case of an investigation from Congress.

In the Spring of 1994, one of my overhead videos revealed a huge hole behind the old power plant. The hole was filled with water. It was a curiousity so I showed it to my friend Tim who is familiar with construction and demolition. After viewing my video tape, he couldn't tell anything at first. Later, he saw another one of my video shots of the same area. This time, the water had dried out, and we could see to the bottom of the hole. Two things showed up. One was a cement structure which was the roof of the underground. The second thing that became apparent was that the hole had not been dug by a machine of any sort. In fact, the hole had the earmarks of being a conduit for water bubbling up from the ground. The pictures indicated that there had been mudslides running down the hill from the big hole.

One Montauk boy (he is a man now) by the name of Mike recalled scuba diving into pockets of water within the Montauk underground. At this point, I realized that the underground must have been flooded. If this is the case, some of the holes dug at Camp Hero could have been dug to rescue people trapped in air pockets of the Montauk underground. Mike could have been diving in order to find the air pockets. Once the people were found, holes could have been dug from the surface. This would be far easier than rescuing them with diving equipment.

The above speculation is one of many indications that a major accident happened in the Montauk underground. I have also noticed that for most of 1994 there have been virtually no transmissions out of Montauk. This accident scenario also explains why the transmissions may have ceased. It could also account for why the Cardion radar was placed above ground. In Chapter One, it was relayed that Mike Nichols was told that the radar had not been working in the underground.

Eye witnesses have also seen very large power amplifiers underground at Montauk. These would require a readily available cooling supply. The particle accelerator would also need cooling water for the cryogenic refrigerators it uses. All of this amounts to a lot of water. What I have heard is that a very large flue in the ocean was constructed in alignment with one of the ocean currents. It is supposedly about a short distance below the ocean at low tide and descends into the ocean about fifty or seventy feet where it then vents to a large pipe. Like a giant

232

funnel in the ocean, it feeds a steady pressure into the pipe that leads right to the underground where the water cools the equipment.

What probably happened is that either due to the demolition work or a general accident, the big pipeline ruptured and flooded the underground. Once the hydrostatic pressure built up enough on the roof of the underground, it went crack and a geyser emerged at the location we know as the big hole. That hole certainly appeared to be a relief point for the water to run out. At the time the hole was filled with water (in the spring of '94), there was water all over Montauk Point that I had never seen before. The swamps were overfilled with water and it was salt water according to reports. I did not personally taste it or test it myself. It is also interesting to note that a lot of vegetation in the swamps is dead. This could be a result of a salt water flood from the underground.

For the time being, this wraps up my case for an underground at Montauk that was flooded with water. I'm sure when the final truth is discovered, it will be far stranger than anything I have offered thus far. And for your own safety, please heed my warning to stay away.

SEALED BUNKER

The Cardion Corporation had set up their operation right in front of
this bunker. Preparations to seal it began soon after Cardion left
the site. According to reports, this bunker eventually leads
to the main underground facilities of Montauk.

LARGE AND SMALL ROCKS

These rocks were photographed just behind the fishermen's cliff.
Some people contend that these rocks are brought
up from the Montauk underground.

32

THE MYSTERY BOTTLE

During one of the video flights over Montauk, another interesting sequence of events happened. As I flew over Camp Hero, a small building the size of a closet appeared amidst the foliage. I once heard of its existence from some kids who were pursued by a black helicopter in the area, but I had never seen it. Something odd began to happen. I could not find it on the viewfinder. It seemed to appear and disappear. It came back again, and I zoomed in on it.

After returning home, I scrutinized the footage of this building very closely. It was one of the few above ground structures at Camp Hero that I had never explored. Slowing down the frames to 1/30th of a second, I saw a square hatch with some sort of shiny round object next to it. The building then disappears and comes back. Next, the shiny object is on a black raised surface next to the rectangular hatch. Suddenly, this black thing rises like a trap door from the roof, but it appears in one frame only. In the very next frame, the roof goes back to its original appearance. No door could open and shut that fast but that something happened on the picture frame is unmistakable. It was time to investigate and get a closer look.

A week later, we mounted a foot trip and went into the lion's den. I was accompanied by Peter Moon and our friend Tim. The little building is not within the inner fence that is guarded by the State Park Police. We were careful not to enter any areas that were marked "no trespassing". Consequently, we followed a very circuitous route through the swamps. Finally, after getting lost for about an hour, we found the building. Upon inspection of the roof, there is no way that anything could have come up and closed in 1/30th of a second. The hatch was indeed a hatch, but it was much smaller than the black thing that appeared to rise in the video frame.

Mysteriously, there was a ladder right next to the building. This didn't make any sense as there was no apparent reason to climb the little building. Peter put the ladder up and stepped onto the roof for a quick second but almost fell through. There is no way a person could have been atop the building when the video footage was shot.

All three of us saw an unusual looking wine bottle on the roof of the building. It was filled with dirty water. I video taped it along with the rest of the roof. When I returned home and viewed the footage of the building, I could not find the wine bottle on the video. This was odd. The next morning it showed up in the mud room of my house. I showed it to Peter and Tim and it looked like the same bottle we had seen earlier. It didn't make any sense. What happened here?

It's been suggested that this was the group at Montauk saying, "Here, look what we can do."

One theory is that when the building disappeared, there was a very local reality shift and another building came in that had some sort of black thing that looked like an opened door. The theory is, that this mechanical thing would come up very fast through the building, vent something from the underground and sink back down again. The only explanation for that would be an alternate reality. This footage will be available on my video tape, Montauk Tour, Part II. For now, we have to add it to the list of Montauk enigmas.

33

THE MONTAUK BOYS

In *Montauk Revisited* we told the story of the Montauk Boys. These are boys who were used for various underhanded activity during the Montauk Project. They were generally Aryan in appearance and were often kidnapped or lured into the project by other means. They were usually abused and programmed with psychosexual techniques. Their programming primarily consisted of going out into society and serving the agenda of the secret government. Often, they were sent out in a sleeper capacity. The idea was for them to attain normal positions in society and be prepared to assume key positions in a military dictatorship if things were to deteriorate into martial law.

I believe that most of the boys during the original Montauk Project had the life whipped right out of them. The idea was to drive the spirit out of the body and make it programmable. If it took brutality, so be it. Later on in my investigation, younger Montauk boys surfaced who showed no sign of beatings or trauma. It has since been learned from deprogramming the Montauk boys that the Montauk boy project went through a transition stage. First, they started out beating the boys. They later learned that there were other and better physical means of getting the soul right out of the body.

The set up they used to recruit the boys became much more humane as well. If you take almost any young boy, and tell them that they'll be working for the United States, they are probably happy with the country. While they are recruiting the boys, they are also testing them and educating them. In the times in between, the boys are shown a good time with recreational facilities and what not. The idea was to get them to volunteer. They were told they were going to go through hell, but when they got through they'd be part of an elite group on the planet. The boys were not only given a rap about being amongst the avant garde of the planet, they might even save the planet itself.

In this manner, most of the boys volunteered. The only time they were brutalized was if they were part of the project and none of the other metaphysical means would work. But that became the rarity. If they couldn't get a subject out of the body by metaphysical means, and he was just a run of the mill boy, they would just erase his memories and send him back.

As part of the recreational angle, game rooms and meeting rooms were set up for the boys. Treated like VIPs, they were given free roam over the first level of the underground which became their level. We understand that although it was somewhat rustic, the first level of underground was redesigned to be pleasant. Some of the boys still remember the boys bunker as opposed to what I just said. This suggests that the Montauk boys bunker is still active in another reality. We've since learned that Montauk has a reality bridge and that a lot of activity at Montauk is in alternate realities.

I have since found that the majority of the boys were part of what we call the Delta Force, a group that goes in and recovers UFOs. Sometimes these are in the U.S. or another part of the planet. Other times they are in another reality. These boys are men today and are highly trained to go in and battle the aliens. This information comes from various people I've worked with who say that their job is to go in and literally play Rambo. Of course, its not hard to find boys who want to go in and be Rambo. These men have literally been trained for years to be part of this very elite group. They are generally very happy to do the work but are programmed not to remember it in their regular lives because it is top top secret.

One of the fellows I worked with was angry because he went into the army and knew he had a very important position but was still treated like any other army grunt. He was actually mistreated, but he knew there was another part of his service where he was actually treated like top dog. These Delta Force people were treated as an elite group when they were in the service thereof. But because their function goes far beyond what could be considered a normal military scenario, one can understand why they would be programmed to forget their activities. The following example will illustrate this point.

While deprogramming one of the boys, I heard some commotion outside and felt the presence of someone in my yard. I chased this guy all around but couldn't see him. I could hear him and even saw him bend branches when he went by the bushes. This man was invisible. This might sound outrageous but it is actually an outgrowth of the Philadelphia Experiment that has taken decades to develop. A number of boys in the Delta Force say they wear a personal invisibility unit that is about the size of a small portable tape recorder and fits on the belt. The unit has three settings: off, invisible and gone. In "off" mode, you are in the environment and are invisible. When the setting is set at "invisible", you can't be seen visually nor are you detectable by light or radar, but you can do physical interaction in this reality. The third setting is "gone". This means you are in a parallel reality and can just view into this reality. You don't have any effect in this reality except to see it. In this manner, you can literally walk through walls. This is obviously a massive capability that these guys have.

For those of you who have seen my video tape *The Montauk Tour*, I believe we have video recorded one of these guys. As I am turning around a bend in the road, he turns it on and starts phasing out within the frames of the video.

Not all of the Montauk boys were set up to work in the Delta Force. There are other sites across the country and the entire program is probably loaded with different agendas and surprises. I began to discover this first hand when I met a man in Seattle. He had an implant that was roaring out a signal. It was resonating over his body, and I could actually feel it. Anyone with the slightest sensitivities would likely have noticed the signal too. It reminded me of a radio signal but was actually a higher order signal. I realized this guy was transmitting.

I soon began working with this gentleman who I will refer to as Bill. Soon it dawned on me that I had actually designed Bill's implant while I was working at Montauk. I discovered that I could psychically control the implant and shut it off and on. When I turned it off, Bill started to pass out so I turned it back on. Although I am neither a computer programmer or technician, I knew the computer language for this implant and it enabled me to break one of my own memory blocks.

After this discovery with Bill, I decided to look for other implants as well. Mike Ash was the next one to be checked. At first, none were apparent. As I checked deeper, I would eventually find that Mike's implant was rigged to shut down whenever someone were to probe for it. First, I had theorized that Mike had an implant. I then attempted to control it psychically and found that I was able to turn it on. I could even feel the transmissions.

As I continued to research, I found that Bill's implant had a malfunction where it wouldn't shut down when you probed for it. That's how I stumbled across it. Mike's shut down program worked, but I was able to ride over it.

The implant itself has a Central Processing Unit or CPU. That's a chip that is usually in the breast bone, right over the heart. Just below the CPU is the memory chip. This sits below the implant at the bottom of the rib cage. Right around the back of the neck is an interface which connects to a maze of wires that goes into the back of the head.

This is organized by a group of electrodes that are implanted into the nerves. There are actually five electrodes for each nerve, but I will only describe three because two are simply reverse directions of what I'm describing. The first electrode picks up the neurological impulse on the nerve fiber of the neuron. The second electrode generates the exact opposite impulse and cancels it. The third electrode injects the impulse or a new impulse from the computer. Everything is literally "neuro-net wired" to go through the computer.

The computer has some programming of its own, but the computer also connects to a data transceiver which means that from a distance, one can literally look through the eyes and senses of the boys. At the same time, they can send a signal back to the implant to change the signal content on the neuro-net. This is control of a lower basic kind. They're controlling the physical thoughts and what this guy is doing physically. It is a very very sophisticated technique.

This type of implant must be performed only when the brain is fully developed which occurs sometime during puberty. The exact timing is relative to the individual. This partly explains the wide variation of age in boys they brought in to the Montauk Project. Not every boy has a fully developed brain at exactly the same age. They had to find the point where each individual was fully developed neurologically. If the implant were installed with regard to the above guidelines, it wouldn't have to be changed for the rest of the individual's life.

Implants are a front line of technology that the Montauk crew uses to manipulate. By studying them we can better defend ourselves against those who might wish you to do us harm. I also understand that many people will be horrified when they read the intricate nature of these devices. The most important thing to remember in all of this is that implants are only effective if the host agrees to them. It is possible to free yourself from anything.

34

MONTAUK
TRANSMISSIONS

The Montauk underground and the programming of the boys are just two threads of evidence that suggest that the Montauk Project is still active today. There is also the matter of transmissions emanating from the area of Camp Hero.

Although transmissions from Montauk were rather quiet after the flooding incident, there was quite a bit of activity in 1993. On August 15th of that year, I made a field trip to Montauk Point. I was accompanied by Duncan Cameron, Al Bielek, Pete Sokol, Mike Nichols and Peter Moon. They all witnessed the events I am about to describe.

At approximately 4 P.M. Eastern Daylight Time, we had set up a monitoring station in my van at the "Overlook" which is very close to the old Montauk Air Force Station. Immediately, transmissions could be observed on the oscilloscope. Not surprisingly, the broadcasts were in the range of 420-450 Megahertz. This is the same frequency used for mind control experiments as described in *The Montauk Project: Experiments in Time*. Additionally, other transmissions were picked up in the vicinity of 172-173 Megahertz. This infringes on Channel 7 (ABC) whose guard band is 172-174 Megahertz (to be precise, the carrier frequency is 174 MH). This is illegal. Many people in Montauk have reported interference with Channel 7, but most Montaukians have cable so that ABC TV comes through to them without interference. Using a standard radio direction finder, it was obvious that the signals were emanating from the direction of the old Montauk Air Force Station. I have recorded the above information which will be very convincing to a trained observer.

All of the above points to one more can of worms at Montauk. The old Air Force Station is supposedly a New York State Park. Why would state workers be transmitting anything? Both myself and Peter Moon were told personally by the Park Superintendent that no one could enter the base because of asbestos and PCB removal. Are they perhaps using radio waves to remove the asbestos and oil?

In a further oddity, a refurbished guard station was observed en route to the inner base. Additionally, there was a new gate requiring both a key and a coded access. Not coincidentally, this beefing up of security was accompanied by another strange scenario. A few weeks prior to August 12th (the 10th anniversary of the culmination of the Montauk Project), a brand new radar facility was witnessed on the cliffs south of the base. This is the Cardion radar setup that was mentioned in Chapter One of this book.

A talk between Peter Moon and one of the New York State Park Police revealed that the gate to the inner base had been furnished by the Cardion corporation. According to Peter, the policeman seemed to be purposely vague on the details but said some sort of deal had been worked out. He wasn't sure exactly what. When Peter asked if Cardion had provided the gate in return for using the base, the policeman wouldn't admit to that but just repeated that some sort of deal had been worked out.

This entire scenario prompts some very intriguing questions? First, why was a state park facility being used by private industry? Second, why were illegal signals being broadcast from the vicinity of Radar Hill (where the transmitter building sits — which, by the way, was not in the vicinity of the Cardion radar installation)? Third, why were these transmissions between 420 and 450 Megahertz, the same frequencies used for mind control experiments? Fourth, why is a defunct base supplied with high powered transmission lines, 20 Megawatts of power (this is enough power to run a small city) and new telephone lines? At the same time, we were being told by the highest ranking park official out there that the base was being dismantled.

These are not new questions as they have been observed for a long time, but this is the first time they have appeared in book form. In the past, ham radio operators have complained to the FCC of illegal frequencies emanating from Montauk. When the FCC has done their investigations, they claim no such transmissions were observed. On the surface, this appears to be either a lazy or dishonest effort by someone in the FCC. If they are going to do a proper investigation, they would have to be impartial and scrutinize the area without first phoning the Montauk operators and telling them to turn it off. For the time being though, everyone is off the hook. The transmissions have not been noticed in 1994. Maybe they got more cautious after this information was published in the 1993 Summer Edition of *The Montauk Pulse*. After all, we had challenged the FCC and local politicians to do an investigation or be named in a lawsuit for allowing improper use of a state park. If these same transmission reoccur, we will be ready for them.

35

THE PARTICLE
ACCELERATOR

It was earlier mentioned in this book that a particle accelerator had been discovered as a result of me doing a video fly-by of Camp Hero. What appeared to be a large circle cut out of the foliage was identified as a particle accelerator by my friend Danny, a nuclear physicist. I was showing him overhead videos I'd taken of the base. He got excited and asked me to freeze the frame. He then pulled out a diagram of a particle accelerator, held it up to the screen and began to identify the various parts of a particle accelerator.

"Here is the beam line. Here is the maintenance port. Here is the cryogenics (the science that deals with the production of very low temperatures and their effect on the properties of matter) port. Down here is the particle injection point."

If one were to overlay Danny's particle accelerator diagram on my video screen, it would fit exactly where the Montauk circle appeared.

All of this sheds a new light on the Montauk Project. I began to research accordingly and studied particle accelerators. What I found was that a very large particle accelerator is used to feed smaller ones. I believe the larger one to be located at Brookhaven National Labs. Because of the energetic interactions that occur between the different accelerators, the smaller ones have to be located some distance from the main one.

Montauk and the eastern end of Long Island were chosen as an ideal location for the smaller accelerators.

Next, I will explain how this system of particle accelerators works. If you are not technically minded, you might wish to skip the rest of this chapter.

The process begins with the injection of protons into the large accelerator. A proton is a positively charged particle within the nucleus of an atom. It is the antithesis of an electron. For the purposes of the accelerator, the protons were generated by stripping the electrons off of hydrogen atoms. First, they separated the light hydrogen from the heavy hydrogen. This gave them light hydrogen with no neutrons in the nucleus. It is then very easy to strip off the electron off of the hydrogen atom and given it a positive charge. It would then be a proton. A proton stream was then injected into the large accelerator and the protons would begin to accelerate. The protons generated would expand and begin to take up more space until they became more and more virtual.

At the output point of the large accelerator, the protons were travelling at about .5C (C = the speed of light, so .5C is half the speed of light). From the output point, the protons were sent down a magnetically focused tunnel and injected into the accelerator ring on the Montauk base itself. It would then be further accelerated to the speed of light.

What you are doing at the speed of light is taking advantage of the Albert Einstein formula that says energy is equal to mass times the velocity of light squared ($E=MC^2$). The reason this is significant is that a particle at the speed of light is going to have a certain amount of energy based upon the mass/velocity relationship in Einstein's equation, the other form of which can be stated $E=MV^2$ where V stands for velocity. The maximum velocity is the speed of light so the maximum energy is where V is replaced by C.

The whole idea of a particle accelerator is that you are getting a unit of electromagnetic energy (a proton, which acts like a particle) to continually increase its velocity. As the particles are converted to the speed of light, vast amounts of energy are released because you are going from the real world to a totally imaginary world which could also be defined as mental energy.

As I continued to study the particle accelerator at Montauk with Dan, all sorts of alarm bells and light bulbs were set off in my head because it enabled me to explain a problem I'd been encountering for years. Whenever I asked different psychics to read how much power they had at Montauk, they would invariably come up with an astronomical amount: a million megawatts of energy. This didn't make any sense because if you're going to run an amplifier of one million megawatts, it will require at least two million megawatts of power. There isn't enough power on Long Island to run the thing.

When I communicated this to Dan, he had already explained to me what I have just relayed about the different particle accelerators attaining the speed of light. I then asked him how much energy one of these particle accelerators could produce upon attaining the speed of light. Dan then grabbed a chart which had a number of things on it including energy output in comparison to circular diameters of accelerators. We had already measured the Montauk circle as having a 625 foot diameter. Sure enough, on Dan's chart we found one of the entries to be 625 feet. Was that a mere coincidence?

We estimated the other items from the chart, including the diameter of the beam and the energy being put into it. Dan did some figuring and said that the particle accelerator at Montauk was equivalent to a hundred megaton nuclear device. He then went to another chart to find out what a hundred megatons converts to in terms of power. It equaled one million megawatts of power, the same amount different psychics had read.

I began to discover more about particle accelerators after my meeting with Dan. I came across a number of reports of very large power amplifiers being built for particle accelerators. They were designed to operate at 435 Megahertz which means they probably found their way out to Montauk. These power amplifiers were called klystrons and replaced the huge amplitrons used in the underground. This was obviously an engineering decision because two or three klystrons could do the work of 24 amplitrons. They are easier to power and act similarly to a magnetron except that they are linear with no orbit. (A magnetron is a microwave signal source similar to that in a microwave oven. It consists of a tube with an electron orbit that produces vast amounts of RF energy.) Klystrons consist of a tube of about 100 feet long and 20 feet in diameter and are essentially a high powered microwave amplifier that drives the particle beam accelerator.

In the particle beam amplifier (which is the same as saying particle beam accelerator), they use atomic particles like neutrons and protons instead of electrons (which are used in a magnetron or amplitron). The protons/neutrons are then focused into an orbit so that a resonant action occurs in the cavities of the accelerator. A cavity is a resonant space which is bounded by a reflective surface of RF energy such as a metal plate or shielded surface. It is physically resonant based upon the velocity, in this case the speed of light.

These neutrons/protons were specially grouped in their orbit so as to act like energy packets in a magnetron or amplitron (which both have orbiting electrons). As the particles in the particle accelerator were sent around the circle at Montauk, thus approaching the speed of light, the cavity would group with the atomic particles into energy packets. The cavity is then resonating with the energy from the particles. When the electron beam is accelerated further, it imparts energy into the cavities and that translates into output.

The particle accelerator already has a particle orbit. The trick is to somehow group the particles in terms of relativistic phase velocity. If this is done, as the particle beam is approaching the speed of light, you could then literally tap the energy out of the particle accelerator with a group of cavities just like in a magnetron.

Within the particle beam amplifier that includes the 625 foot diameter circle at Montauk, two sets of cavities are positioned at right angles to each other surrounding a circle. Using the output of about a 30 megawatt transmitter, you drive one group of cavities on one of the axis which we'll call the X axis. Just as in a regular amplitron, the input power groups the electron beam spinning around in the amplitron with one set of cavities. This is called slow wave structure (slow wave refers to particles travelling below the speed of light). In the particle beam amplifier, we're not dealing with slow wave but with light velocity wave structure. The input cavities then group the particle beam at about .9 C.

As the particle is accelerated faster and reaches C, it is going to release all the energy. The energy will then be released upon the bunched particles and the Y cavity will then pick up the energy. It is positioned 90° away from the X cavity and conducts the energy in whatever manner has been set.

In order to output the energy from the particle amplifier, it would be normal to put it into wave guides and send it back to the radar tower. But, this won't work because with a million megawatts the wave guides would melt. Instead of taking the energy out of the particle beam amplifier as an energy beam, they allowed the particle beam amplifier to become the antenna. The E field antenna which coupled in with the Delta T antenna was actually the circle of the particle beam amplifier which has an output power of a million megawatts. This is definitely enough to bend space and time.

They constructed the output cavity to go to some sort of rectifier which I still don't fully understand at this point. Some of this energy was used to drive the Delta T antenna, the top tip of which is just below the center of the ground. The bottom tip is way below the center of the ground and under the particle accelerator. To power the X and Y coils of the Delta T, they tapped the particle accelerator just above the ground. They then drove the Z coil, possibly as a white noise source, from the particle accelerator in the main town of Montauk (the traffic circle in the center of town). It is my supposition that they may have gotten some of that energy accelerated to the speed of light. Since the output from the accelerator in town was not modulated, it would be white noise and would serve as the correlating signal for bending time (reference Chapter 12 of

The *Montauk Project*).

Bending time is not the only use of the particle accelerator. It is also used today as a particle beam weapon. It is known that UFOs are sensitive to 435 Megahertz with a 20 Megahertz band width. This is accomplished by using one set of cavities to bunch the particle beam at 435 MH. Then they will used the particle beam port with reflective mirrors and magnetic focusing to launch this thing as a particle beam weapon. When they do this, they generate two interlacing helical beams, very similar to the caduceus function. By controlling the phasing beams, they can control how far out they'll travel and at some point a destructive interference will occur. The beams will destroy each and in turn create an interference which will generate a miniature black hole. Modulation is the key to getting through the shield of the UFO which has been well known since the days of the early Sage radar when they began shooting down UFOs. That is another story, and I am currently working on a book that will explain my experience in the field of UFOs.

36

THE TIME LINE

Most of what I write about Montauk is either technical or experiential, but I would like to end with a philosophical overview with regard to our consciousness of time.

I discovered a number of years ago that the Montauk Project connected with a number of other space-time projects. These, in turn, connected back to other projects that extended throughout history and into the future. It appears that the Montauk Project itself reached directly back to 3.6 million years in the past and to about 6037 in the future. They fed these times back on themselves. What this means is that we actually lived this time line twice. It is the second run through, and quite possibly, we may have been through this time line more than twice. Because we really can't have two different time lines for the same time period, it means that one time line must veer off and become an alternate reality. All of this suggests that the first time line was the time line that God created. The alternate time line is what became original sin.

What exactly is original sin?

If you read the Bible, original sin is the sin of knowledge. That is quite literally what the translations say. We received knowledge and God supposedly kicked us out of the Garden of Eden. He did not kick us out. What happened is when we fed the first time line in on itself, that time line skewed off into an alternate reality and we went into a second time line. The second time line is our creation, not God's. The original God, God the Father, is not on this time line. This is the reason the modern Christian data base is saying that we can reach God the Father through Christ.

What is Christ?

Christ is the piece of us that leads back to God the Father. The cross represents the crossing of our time line with the creator's time line. We can go through this Christ relationship to get back to God the Father who was the original creator. All of this says that original sin is the knowledge of space and time and that we can play God and create our own reality. Of course, we went into that reality and that is how we are separated from our Creator.

There was a collective consciousness that built all these various space-time projects that are all part of the original sin. We now know it as history. Only by becoming conscious of the original time line can we blow off the false time. That is the purpose of these Montauk books.

The mathematics are supposed to be that if ten percent of the beings in this galaxy can become conscious of the original time line, then all beings will follow suit. Hopefully, your consciousness has been raised by the reading of this book. If so, your journey home has begun.

EPILOGUE

The entire scope and synchronicities surrounding Montauk have far exceeded anyone's expectations. Neither Preston nor myself originally had any idea that so many connections would unravel through investigating the subject.

As with all of our research, our best strategy has been to put forth what we find in a book and circulate it so as to acquire further information. In some respects, we are still scratching the surface.

There is no doubt that people will clamor for more information on Montauk and its related phenomena. It is also inevitable that we will continue to investigate and gather information. Accordingly, I will update you on plans for future books.

Preston and I have already been collaborating on a book about his alien experiences. This book will be pure Preston Nichols and is intended to be a ground breaking work on the whole UFO phenomena. It will include a dissertation on UFO technology, abduction phenomena and many other related subjects. With good luck, this publication will be ready by the end of 1995.

There are also several other possible books to write in the future. These would include the following subjects: Jack Parsons and the Babalon Working, the Nazi connection to Montauk/Tibet and the story of Duncan Cameron. Preston also informed me that after reading Part I of this book that he might like to do a book on the last eight days of the Montauk Project. This would center on the connections between Mars and Montauk, part of which was touched on in *Montauk Revisited.* There is considerable research to do on his end before this could even be considered.

And then, there is the movie. People frequently ask if there is going to be a movie about the Montauk Project. We should tell you that there has been definite interest from different sources in Hollywood concerning a motion picture about Montauk. Unfortunately, most of the people who have contacted us in this regard are naive when it comes to dealing with the subject matter. They do not realize that Montauk heads the media's list of subjects to be censored. You can easily understand the sort of difficulty this presents. It is just a matter of time before the world is ready for "Montauk the Movie", and I'm sure all will unfold in its due course.

There are no plans at this time to do a direct follow up on the sacred geometry and mystery school teachings alluded to in this book. For those who are sincerely interested in getting to the bottom of this mysterious universe, I sincerely recommend the study of Stan Tenon's work described in Chapter 10. That is a completely academic approach to the science of sacred geometry and will provide lots of enlightenment.

Of course, any of these plans are subject to change by reason of new breakthroughs on the Montauk front. There is also sure to be some interesting news on the Montauks' quest to regain their native land. This and other developments will continue to be reported on in *The Montauk Pulse* newsletter.

In the meantime, we can all do our own part to assure that as much accurate and sensible information as possible is pumped into the morphogenetic grid. This is simply the process of becoming aware and making others aware.

Finally, it is our sincere hope that this book has taught you something you didn't know before and has raised your consciousness concerning the processes of creation. May your ensuing time line be a pleasant one.

▲

BIBLIOGRAPHY

Alesiter Crowley and the Hidden God, Kenneth Grant, Skoob Books Publishing, London ©1973, 1992

Atlantis: The Eigth Continent by Charles Berlitz G.P. Putnam's Sons, New York ©1984

Geneset Target Earth by David Wood & Ian Campbell, Bellevue Books, London ©1994

The Gods of Eden by William Bramley, Avon Books, New York ©1989, 1990

Guide to Mars by Patrick Moore, W.W. Norton & Company, Inc., New York © 1977

The Magical Revival, Kenneth Gran, Skoob Books Publishing, London ©1972, 1991

Mars At Last! Mark Washburn, G.P. Putnam's Sons, New York ©1977

Mars Beckons, John Noble Wilford, Alfred A. Knopf, New York ©1990

The Nazis and the Occult by Dusty Sklar, Dorset Press, New York ©1977

The Occult Conspiracy by Michael Howard, Destiny Books, Rochester, Vermont ©1989

Portable Darkness by Schott Michaelsen, Harmony Books, New York ©1989

The Secrets of Aleister Crowley by Amado Crowley, Diamond Books ©1991

Serpent in the Sky by John Anthony West, Harper & Row, New York ©1979

Various selected works of Aleister Crowley

Do you know someone who hasn't read the first 2 books?

Give a friend the original book that is still shocking the world. "The Montauk Project: Experiments in Time" chronicles the most amazing and secretive research project in recorded history. After the Philadelphia Experiment of 1943, forty years of massive research ensued, culminating in bizarre experiments at Montauk Point that tapped the powers of creation and actually manipulated time itself. Illustrations, photos and diagrams, 160 pages. See order form on last page.

And the sequel that reveals the occult forces underlying the technology used in the Montauk Project. "Montauk Revisited: Adventures in Synchronicity" carries forward with the Montauk investigation as Preston Nichols opens the door to Peter Moon and unleashes a host of incredible characters and new information. A startling scenario is depicted that reaches far beyond the scope of the first book. Illustrations and photos, 256 pages. See order form.

SkyBooks ORDER FORM

Item	Qty	Cost
The Montauk Project: Experiments in Time..........$15.95		
Montauk Revisited: Adventures in Synchronicity..$19.95		
Pyramids of Montauk: Explorations in Consciousness..................$19.95		
The Montauk Pulse (1 year subscription).............$12.00		
The Montauk Pulse Back Issues (List issues in the space below)..........$3.00 each		
Subtotal		
For delivery in Ny add 8.5% tax		
Shipping: see chart		
U.S. only: Priority mail		
Total		

▼ List **Pulse back issues** (the first newsletter was Winter '93 — and is issued quarterly)

Ship to:

United States Shipping

Under $30.00.....................add $3.00
$30.00 — 60.00.................add $4.00
$60.01 —100.00...............add $6.00
Over $100.00......................add $8.00

Allow 4-6 weeks for delivery. A money order instead of a check will speed delivery. For U.S. only: Priority mail— add the following to the regular shipping charge: $3.00 for first item, $1.50 for each additional item.

Foreign Countries & Canada

Under $30.00......................add $8.00
$30.00 — 60.00...............add $11.00
$60.01 — 100.00..............add $15.00
Over $100.00......................add $20.00

These rates are for SURFACE SHIPPING ONLY. Due to the vastly different costs for each country, we can only ship by surface, not by air. Only postal money orders or checks drawn on a U.S. bank, in U.S. funds will be accepted.

Send money order or check payable to: Sky Books, Box 769, Westbury, Ny 11590-0104